Hyper-V Network Virtualization Cookbook

Over 20 recipes to ease the creation of new virtual
machines in the networking layer using Hyper-V
Network Virtualization

Ryan Boud

PUBLISHING

professional expertise distilled

BIRMINGHAM - MUMBAI

Hyper-V Network Virtualization Cookbook

First published: November 2014

Production reference: 1221114

Published by Packt Publishing Ltd.
Livery Place
35 Livery Street
Birmingham B3 2PB, UK.

ISBN 978-1-78217-780-7

www.packtpub.com

Credits

Author
Ryan Boud

Reviewers
Niklas Akerlund
Markus Darda
James Preston
Lai Yoong Seng

Acquisition Editor
James Jones

Content Development Editor
Sumeet Sawant

Technical Editors
Madhuri Das
Rohit Kumar Singh

Copy Editors
Roshni Banerjee
Merilyn Pereira

Project Coordinator
Aboli Ambardekar

Proofreaders
Simran Bhogal
Maria Gould
Steve Maguire

Indexer
Mariammal Chettiyar

Graphics
Abhinash Sahu

Production Coordinator
Arvindkumar Gupta

Cover Work
Arvindkumar Gupta

About the Author

Ryan Boud has been working in the IT field since 1998 when he started working part-time on a service desk while studying at Goldsmiths College, University of London. After graduating, he worked his way up to manage the customer IT service desk. He then moved into IT management and development, creating internal applications and middleware for third-party applications. Recently, Ryan moved to Inframon, The Cloud Transformation Specialists, as a System Center and Desktop Implementation Consultant. He has worked on numerous different implementations of Microsoft Windows Server 2012 R2 Hyper-V and System Center 2012 R2 for a variety of customers in the public and private sectors.

I would like to thank James, Sumeet, and others at Packt Publishing for all their assistance in writing this book. Additionally, I would like to thank the technical reviewers for their fantastic feedback and guidance.

I would especially like to thank Gordon and Sean at Inframon whose belief in me has encouraged me to take this opportunity to write a book, which has always been on my list of career goals.

My final thanks go to my wife, Sarah, who has always believed in me and has helped keep our children busy while I was writing this book! Additionally, I would like to thank her for all her support; without her, I wouldn't be able to do the job I love doing and have wanted to do for so long.

About the Reviewers

Niklas Akerlund works as Chief Technical Architect - Microsoft Solutions at a consultancy firm in Sweden. He has extensive experience in design and adoption of hybrid cloud solutions with Hyper-V, Azure, Office 365, and EMS. He also works on the design, implementation, and upgrading of private clouds using MS Hyper-V 2012 R2 with System Center for customers with a strong focus on automation.

He often writes posts about virtualization and automation on his blog, `http://vniklas.djungeln.se/`; you can follow him on twitter at `http://twitter.com/vniklas`.

Niklas is the cofounder of PowerShell User Group Sweden; he has also been awarded Hyper-V MVP for his contributions to and love for sharing technology with other IT professionals.

Markus Darda is the owner of MD Consultancy, Germany, and DaComp GmbH, Switzerland. As senior Citrix engineer and architect, he works for Enterprise customers all over Europe to design and implement Citrix (XenApp and XenDesktop) environments based on different Hypervisors. As a Citrix and Microsoft trainer, he teaches about Microsoft Server Products and Citrix Products to customers all over Europe. He also works for Citrix as a Subject Matter Expert (SME) in different courseware and exams.

He has worked for Lanxess, Germany; T-Systems, Germany; Koenen en Co, the Netherlands; and other companies in Switzerland, Sweden, and Norway.

He has also worked on *Citrix XenApp® 7.5 Desktop Virtualization Solutions*, *Packt Publishing*, and other different courseware from Citrix.

James Preston is an IT professional working in the education field and has a broad range of interests, including Virtualization with Hyper-V and App-V, data-orientated application design with Visual Studio Lightswitch, IP telephony, and Remote Access technologies.

To share his knowledge, James runs a blog (`http://myworldofit.net/`) that covers a wide range of the most recent topics, including publishing a WebDAV server, the effective integration of student databases with virtual learning environments, and his take on an enterprise Wi-Fi deployment.

When he isn't working, he can be found in the local coffee shop having a go at the latest computer games or planning the training program for his local air cadet squadron.

Lai Yoong Seng is a Microsoft Most Valuable Professional (MVP) in Hyper-V since 2010. He has more than 14 years of IT experience and he joined Hyper-V and System Center Specialist Infront Consulting in Malaysia. He started off by specializing in Microsoft Virtualization, and then started blogging (`www.ms4u.info`) and presenting at local and regional events. He is the founder of Malaysia Virtualization User Group (MVUG), which is a one-stop center for people to learn about Hyper-V, System Center, and Azure.

Previously, he was actively engaged as Technology Early Adopter (TAP) and Tester of System Center Virtual Machine Manager 2012, System Center 2012 SP1, Windows Server 2012 R2 and System Center 2012 R2, and Azure Site Recovery.

Then, he was a technical reviewer for the book *Windows Server 2012 Hyper-V: Deploying Hyper-V Enterprise Server Virtualization Platform* and the video *Building and Managing a Virtual Environment with Hyper-V Server 2012 R2*, both by Packt Publishing.

Reviewing a book takes a lot of effort and is a difficult process. It would not be possible without help from my family, colleagues, and friends. I would like to thank my parents for their understanding, patience, and help to keep all the other stuff together while I was reviewing the a book. In addition, a very special thanks to Packt Publishing for an opportunity to contribute to this book.

www.PacktPub.com

Support files, eBooks, discount offers, and more

For support files and downloads related to your book, please visit www.PacktPub.com.

Did you know that Packt offers eBook versions of every book published, with PDF and ePub files available? You can upgrade to the eBook version at www.PacktPub.com and as a print book customer, you are entitled to a discount on the eBook copy. Get in touch with us at service@packtpub.com for more details.

At www.PacktPub.com, you can also read a collection of free technical articles, sign up for a range of free newsletters and receive exclusive discounts and offers on Packt books and eBooks.

https://www2.packtpub.com/books/subscription/packtlib

Do you need instant solutions to your IT questions? PacktLib is Packt's online digital book library. Here, you can search, access, and read Packt's entire library of books.

Why subscribe?

- Fully searchable across every book published by Packt
- Copy and paste, print, and bookmark content
- On demand and accessible via a web browser

Free access for Packt account holders

If you have an account with Packt at www.PacktPub.com, you can use this to access PacktLib today and view 9 entirely free books. Simply use your login credentials for immediate access.

Instant updates on new Packt books

Get notified! Find out when new books are published by following @PacktEnterprise on Twitter or the *Packt Enterprise* Facebook page.

Table of Contents

Preface

Welcome to *Hyper-V Network Virtualization Cookbook*. This book is an end-to-end introduction on how to implement Hyper-V Network Virtualization (HNV) on Microsoft Windows Server 2012 R2 Hyper-V using System Center 2012 R2 Virtual Machine Manager.

The purpose of this book is to help you get familiar with the components of Hyper-V Network Virtualization and the options available to you. It is assumed that you are familiar with Windows Server 2012 R2 and want to understand how to implement HNV.

Software-defined Networks (SDN) are networks decoupled from the traditional physical hardware. SDN allows IT and network administrators to react to changing business requirements faster as it removes the requirement to amend the physical infrastructure. Microsoft's implementation of SDN uses the NVGRE protocol, which is referred to as Hyper-V Network Virtualization.

What this book covers

Chapter 1, Installing Virtual Machine Manager, shows you how to install Virtual Machine Manager (VMM), which is a critical component of HNV. This chapter discusses the components required for VMM and how to configure them correctly.

Chapter 2, Configuring Networks for Hyper-V Network Virtualization, teaches you the required configurations in VMM for Logical Networks, Virtual Machine Networks (VM Networks), IP Pools, and virtual machines.

Chapter 3, Creating the Gateway for Virtual Machine Communications, demonstrates how to create an HNV gateway and connect it to VM Networks.

Chapter 4, *IP Address Management Integration with VMM for Hyper-V Network Virtualization*, demonstrates how to integrate IPAM with VMM.

Chapter 5, *Windows Server Gateway Configuration*, goes deeper into the capabilities of the Windows Server gateway, showing you how to use the different options for gateways—including Network Address Translation and Direct Routing.

Chapter 6, *Implementing Network Isolation in Hyper-V*, discusses how to implement traditional networking in Hyper-V with regards to VLANs and PVLANs.

Chapter 7, *Network Access Control Lists*, details the options available to Hyper-V administrators for securing their virtual machines. For example, how to control what can access a VM on a specific port and how the Hyper-V Extensible Switch can be used here.

Appendix A, *VM Templates*, will discuss the Virtual Machine Templates, which are created using the `Convert-WindowsImage.ps1` PowerShell script.

Appendix B, *Planning the Virtual Machine Manager*, will help you with the preparation and planning of the Virtual Machine Manager.

What you need for this book

The hardware and software requirements are covered in the following sections.

Hardware requirements

To complete all of the recipes in this book, you will need five computers capable of running Windows Server 2012 R2 Hyper-V each with at least 8 GB RAM. Please ensure that your hardware meet the minimum requirements for Windows Server 2012 R2 and for Hyper-V. Please refer to the TechNet article at `http://technet.microsoft.com/en-us/library/jj647784` for more details.

In addition, you will need a switch capable of IEEE 802.1q VLANs. The following diagram shows you how the hardware should be connected:

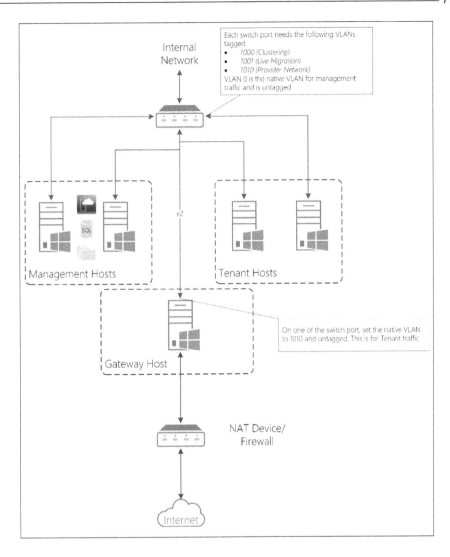

In addition, you will need some shared storage for the Management Hosts and Tenant Hosts to be able to create Hyper-V clusters. The NAT Device / Firewall does not have to offer DHCP addresses, as System Center 2012 R2 Virtual Machine Manager will be responsible for distributing IP addresses for use on this network by Hyper-V Network Virtualization.

Software requirements

All of the recipes in this book are based on the following software:

- ▶ Windows Server 2012 R2
- ▶ System Center 2012 R2 Virtual Machine Manager
- ▶ SQL Server 2012 SP1 Enterprise Edition

It is advisable to ensure that you install the latest Update Rollup available for all products. Microsoft is continually refining the products involved, and it is highly recommended that you have the latest updates installed, the exception being SQL Server 2012. It is advised to install the latest Cumulative Update of Service Pack 1 and not to install Service Pack 2.

The Fully Qualified Domain Name for the Active Directory domain in this book is `ad.demo.com` and the NetBIOS name is DEMO. The functional levels of the Forest and Domain are both Windows Server 2012 R2.

You do not require SQL Server 2012 SP1 Enterprise Edition for Hyper-V Network Virtualization. However, it offers the AlwaysOn High Availability Group function, which offers significantly faster failover in the event of a SQL Server failure. System Center 2012 includes a license for SQL Server 2012 Standard Edition, which is sufficient for most installations.

Who this book is for

The target audience of this book is Network and Virtualization administrators who are responsible for architecting their infrastructure. The recipes in this book will demonstrate how to implement HNV. The ultimate goal of this book is to provide a sound understanding of how HNV can be implemented and the components involved.

Sections

This book contains the following sections:

Getting ready

This section tells us what to expect in the recipe, and describes how to set up any software or any preliminary settings needed for the recipe.

How to do it...

This section characterizes the steps to be followed for "cooking" the recipe.

How it works...

This section usually consists of a brief and detailed explanation of what happened in the previous section.

There's more...

It consists of additional information about the recipe in order to make the reader more anxious about the recipe.

See also

This section may contain references to the recipe.

Conventions

In this book, you will find a number of styles of text that distinguish between different kinds of information. Here are some examples of these styles, and an explanation of their meaning.

Code words in text, database table names, folder names, filenames, file extensions, pathnames, dummy URLs, user input, and Twitter handles are shown as follows: "Enter the FQDN of the IPAM server; in this case, `DEMO-IPAM01.ad.demo.com`."

A block of code is set as follows:

```
Set-PSDrive AD:

$VMMInstallAccount = Get-ADUser -Identity Install_VMM
```

When we wish to draw your attention to a particular part of a code block, the relevant lines or items are set in bold:

```
$logicalNetwork = Get-SCLogicalNetwork -ID "f69abe75-0e94-
    42a9-b86a-6d48c4010c1a"
```

Any command-line input or output is written as follows:

```
Install-WindowsFeature -Name IPAM -IncludeManagementTools
```

New terms and **important words** are shown in bold. Words that you see on the screen, in menus or dialog boxes for example, appear in the text like this: "Click on the **Utilization Trend** tab."

Warnings or important notes appear in a box like this.

Tips and tricks appear like this.

Reader feedback

Feedback from our readers is always welcome. Let us know what you think about this book—what you liked or may have disliked. Reader feedback is important for us to develop titles that you really get the most out of.

To send us general feedback, simply send an e-mail to `feedback@packtpub.com`, and mention the book title via the subject of your message.

If there is a topic that you have expertise in and you are interested in either writing or contributing to a book, see our author guide on `www.packtpub.com/authors`.

Customer support

Now that you are the proud owner of a Packt book, we have a number of things to help you to get the most from your purchase.

Downloading the example code

You can download the example code files for all Packt books you have purchased from your account at `http://www.packtpub.com`. If you purchased this book elsewhere, you can visit `http://www.packtpub.com/support` and register to have the files e-mailed directly to you.

Errata

Although we have taken every care to ensure the accuracy of our content, mistakes do happen. If you find a mistake in one of our books—maybe a mistake in the text or the code—we would be grateful if you would report this to us. By doing so, you can save other readers from frustration and help us improve subsequent versions of this book. If you find any errata, please report them by visiting `http://www.packtpub.com/submit-errata`, selecting your book, clicking on the **Errata Submission Form** link, and entering the details of your errata. Once your errata are verified, your submission will be accepted and the errata will be uploaded on our website, or added to any list of existing errata, under the Errata section of that title. Any existing errata can be viewed by selecting your title from `http://www.packtpub.com/support`.

To view the previously submitted errata, go to `https://www.packtpub.com/books/content/support` and enter the name of the book in the search field. The required information will appear under the **Errata** section.

Piracy

Piracy of copyright material on the Internet is an ongoing problem across all media. At Packt, we take the protection of our copyright and licenses very seriously. If you come across any illegal copies of our works, in any form, on the Internet, please provide us with the location address or website name immediately so that we can pursue a remedy.

Please contact us at `copyright@packtpub.com` with a link to the suspected pirated material.

We appreciate your help in protecting our authors, and our ability to bring you valuable content.

Questions

You can contact us at `questions@packtpub.com` if you are having a problem with any aspect of the book, and we will do our best to address it.

1
Installing Virtual Machine Manager

In this chapter, we will cover the following recipes:

- ▸ Deploying the required service accounts
- ▸ Creating the distributed key management container in Active Directory
- ▸ Installing Virtual Machine Manager on a single server
- ▸ Installing a highly available Virtual Machine Manager server

Introduction

Microsoft System Center 2012 R2 **Virtual Machine Manager** (**VMM**) is a critical component of Hyper-V Network Virtualization. It provides the management infrastructure to control Hyper-V Network Virtualization.

It provides the following features:

- Network definitions, both physical and virtual
- Control of Hyper-V hosts
- Virtual Machine templates
- Service templates

VMM is a part of the Microsoft System Center 2012 R2 product. It is primarily composed of seven components, which are listed in the following table:

VMM component	Description
VirtualManagerDB	VirtualManagerDB is a Microsoft SQL Server database. It contains all the configuration data for VMM, the passwords (encrypted), job history, performance data, and so on.
VMM Console	This console makes use of the VMM PowerShell module to perform all of its tasks. It is purely a frontend for the VMM PowerShell module.
VMM Management Server	The management server is responsible for undertaking all actions. It is responsible for communicating with its agents on Hyper-V hosts, library servers, WSUS servers, and so on.
VMM Library Server	The library server contains all the physical files required for virtual and physical machines, including VHDX files, answer files, drivers for physical servers, application files, and so on.
VMM Agent	This is responsible for undertaking the required actions from the VMM Management Server.
VMM PXE Server	The PXE server is a Windows Deployment server that has the VMM agent server installed. It is solely used for bare metal deployment of Hyper-V hosts.
VMM Update Server	This is a WSUS server that has updates applicable to the servers under VMM's management.

The following diagram shows the components and where they would be installed:

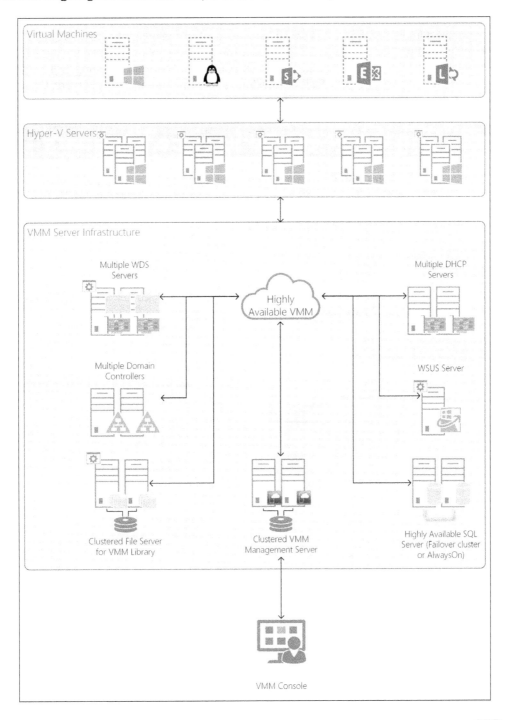

VMM is capable of managing the alternative hypervisors: XenServer and VMware ESX/vSphere (via a VMware vCenter installation).

For the smallest implementation, it is possible to install all of the components on a single server, including the VirtualManagerDB database. You have the option to make the installation of VMM highly available by using features such as SQL Server Failover Clustering, SQL Server AlwaysOn High Availability Groups, Failover Clustering for VMM Management Servers, Clustered File Servers for the VMM Library, and multiple Windows Deployment Servers.

Deploying the required service accounts

This recipe will provide you with the steps required to deploy the required service accounts to the correct servers. It will assist you with your evaluation of Virtual Machine Manager before deploying into a production environment. For the purpose of the Service Accounts, please read *Appendix*, *Planning Virtual Machine Manager*.

Getting ready

It is assumed you have access to Active Directory to create and populate Security Groups and to create and link Group Policy Objects.

How to do it...

The following diagram shows you the high-level steps involved in this recipe and the tasks required to complete this recipe:

Overview of Recipe:

Prerequisites (not covered by this recipe):
- Agree the service account usernames and passwords
- Agree the required Security Group names
- Agree the Organisation Unit structure
- Agree the Group Policy Object names

Actions:
- Creation of required Service Accounts
- Creation of required Security Groups
- Creation of required Group Policy Objects
- Linking Security Groups to Group Policy Objects
- Linking Group Policy Objects to the correct Organisational Units
- Initiating a remote Group Policy Update

The following screenshot shows how the Active Directory **Organization Units** (**OUs**) are structured for this recipe:

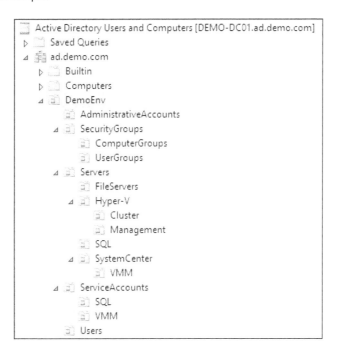

The list of accounts that will be used is as follows:

Account name	Use	Username
VMM Service Account	Running VMM services and accessing resources	SVC_VMMSrvc
VMM Agent Run As Account	Managing Hyper-V Hosts and Infrastructure Servers	SVC_VMMAgntRA
VMM SQL Server Account	Running VMM SQL Server instance	SVC_VMMSQLEng
VMM SQL Server Agent Account	Running VMM SQL Server Agent for a SQL instance	SVC_VMMSQLAgnt
VM Domain Join Run As Account	Joining new VMs to the domain	SVC_VMMJoinDom
VMM Installation Account	The account used to install VMM	Install_VMM

Now perform the following steps:

1. Create the user accounts for VMM.

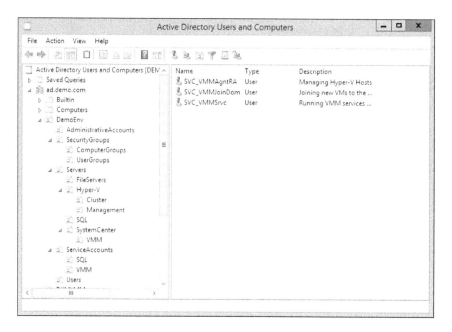

2. The user accounts for SQL are shown in the following screenshot:

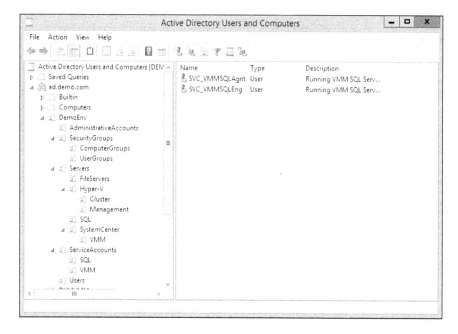

3. The groups for Hyper-V Servers and VMM Servers are shown in the following screenshot:

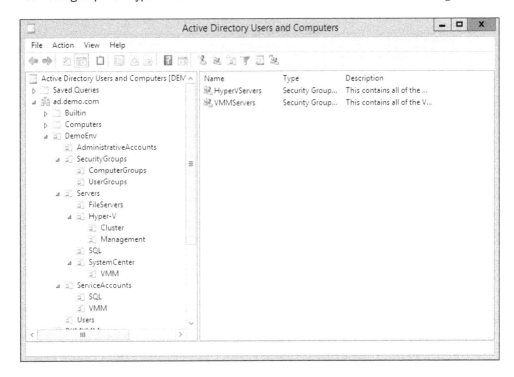

4. A new **Group Policy Object** (**GPO**) needs to be created and linked to the Hyper-V OU.

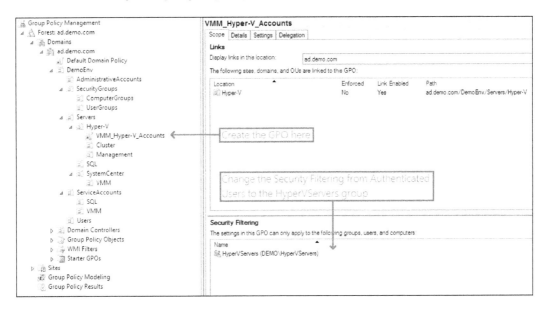

5. Click on the **Details** tab and select **User configuration settings disabled** from the **GPO Status** dropdown, as shown in the following screenshot:

6. Right-click on the GPO name under the Hyper-V OU and click on **Edit**. Navigate to **Computer Configuration | Preferences | Control Panel Settings | Local Users and Groups**. Right-click and navigate to **New | Local Group**.

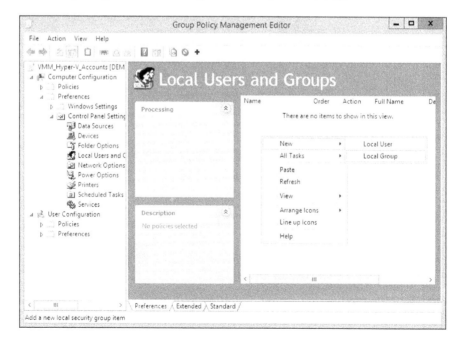

7. Make sure the **Action** field is set to **Update**, **Group name** is set to **Administrators (built-in)**, and you have added **SVC_VMMAgntRA** to the **Members** section.

8. Click on **OK** to close the **New Local Group Properties** dialog.
9. Close the **Group Policy Management Editor** window.

10. In the **Group Policy Management** MMC, right-click on the OU where the GPO has been deployed and click on **Group Policy Update**. This triggers a remote Group Policy Update on the Hyper-V hosts.

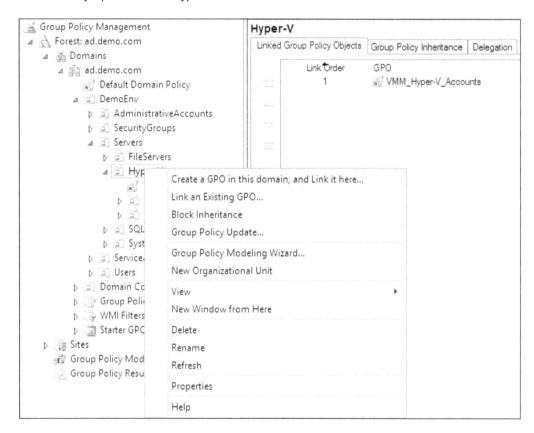

This completes this recipe. The required service accounts with the necessary permissions have been scoped and deployed correctly.

How it works...

By adding the required Service Accounts to the Group Policy Objects, it ensures that these accounts have sufficient privileges to run and manage the VMM installation.

Creating the distributed key management container in Active Directory

Some of the data stored by VMM needs to be held securely, so it cannot be compromised. For example, when you store user credentials in VMM for Run As accounts, the passwords for these are encrypted. When you install VMM, you are given the choice of where to store the encryption keys, as shown in the following screenshot:

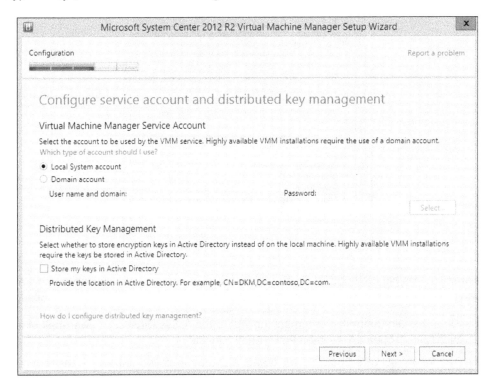

It is required to always store your encryption keys in Active Directory if you are going to deploy a highly available (clustered) installation of VMM.

The account used to install VMM must have full control over the container in Active Directory for the duration of the installation. During the installation, the installer program reconfigures the security of the container to ensure that only the correct security principles have access.

For a small scale installation, a single container in the root of Active Directory could be created to store the encryption keys. For a large-scale implementation where several different installations of VMM may be required due to the number of hosts and/or virtual machines, it is advisable to create a parent container in Active Directory and then have containers within the parent for each installation of VMM.

Getting ready

You will need to have sufficient access to Active Directory to create Container objects.

How to do it...

The following diagram shows you the high-level steps involved in this recipe and the tasks required to complete this recipe:

```
Overview of Recipe:

    Prerequisites (not covered by this recipe):
    • Obtaining an account with sufficient privileges for
      creating a container in Active Directory
    • Obtaining an account with sufficient privileges for
      changing ACLs on the new container in Active
      Directory

    Actions:
    • Creation of new container in Active Directory for
      Distributed Key Management in VMM using
      PowerShell
    • Applying the required security permissions to the
      newly created Active Directory container using
      PowerShell
```

There are two possible methods of creating a container in Active Directory: one is using ADSI Edit and the other is via PowerShell. The method discussed here will be PowerShell-based:

1. On a Domain Controller, or a machine where the Active Directory PowerShell Module is installed, open an elevated PowerShell console.

2. The following PowerShell line will create a container called DKMVMM in the root of Active Directory:

    ```
    New-ADObject -Name DKMVMM -Type container -Path
        "DC=ad,DC=demo,DC=com"
    ```

3. Once the container has been created, the user who will be installing VMM needs to have full control of the container and that permission must apply to the container and all descendant objects. The following PowerShell will perform this function:

```
Set-PSDrive AD:

$VMMInstallAccount = Get-ADUser -Identity Install_VMM

$SID = New-Object
   System.Security.Principal.SecurityIdentifier
      $VMMInstallAccount.SID

$DKMVMMacl = Get-Acl -Path "CN=DKMVMM,DC=ad,DC=demo,DC=com"

$ObjectGuid = New-Object Guid 00000000-0000-0000-0000-
   000000000000

$newACL = New-Object
   System.DirectoryServices.ActiveDirectoryAccessRule
      $SID,"GenericAll","Allow",$objectguid,"All"

$DKMVMMacl.AddAccessRule($newACL)

Set-Acl -AclObject $DKMVMMacl -Path
   "CN=DKMVMM,DC=ad,DC=demo,DC=com"
```

This recipe is complete and the Distributed Key Management container is now ready to be used by DEMO\Install_VMM during installation.

How it works...

When VMM is installed, it uses the Distributed Key Management container to store its encryption keys and using the privileges granted to it previously, it will lock down the container to ensure that only the account running the VMM Management Service, the VMM Installation Account, and Domain Administrators have access to the container.

Installing Virtual Machine Manager on a single server

This recipe provides the steps required to install all the VMM roles on a single server, including SQL Server. This type of deployment is suitable for the test and development environments. It will enable you to evaluate VMM for Hyper-V Network Virtualization. While supported, it is highly recommended that a multiserver deployment is implemented for production. A multiserver installation can give you a great deal of flexibility and resiliency in a VMM installation.

Getting ready

It is assumed you have reviewed the recipe and have implemented the required elements for installing VMM.

How to do it...

The following diagram shows you the high-level steps involved in this recipe and the tasks required to complete this recipe:

Overview of Recipe:

Prerequisites (not covered by this recipe):
- Obtaining the SQL Server and VMM ISO files
- Creation of a virtual machine for SQL and VMM

Actions:
- Adding the .NET 3.5 Framework to Windows Server 2012 R2
- Installing SQL Server 2012 SP1
- Installing VMM 2012 R2

This will result in the following applications and their components being installed on this single server:

- SQL Server 2012 SP1 for the VirtualManagerDB database
- VMM 2012 R2 Management Server with the VMM Console and VMM Library

To install VMM, you must install SQL Server 2008 R2 SP2 or higher. This recipe will discuss installing SQL Server 2012 SP1 Standard Edition, which is included in the System Center license.

.NET Framework

SQL Server 2012 requires the .NET 3.5 Framework. The source files for this are not installed on a Windows Server 2012 (or higher) installation by default. To add the .NET 3.5 Framework, you will need access to the Windows Server 2012 R2 DVD/ISO content.

The following PowerShell must be executed from an elevated PowerShell console:

```
Install-WindowsFeature -Name Net-Framework-Core -Source
  D:\sources\sxs
```

> D: denotes where the ISO contents are available from. This could be a network share if more appropriate for you.

VMM requires .NET Framework 4.5 (or 4.5.1) and is installed on Windows Server 2012 R2 by default.

Downloading the example code

You can download the example code files for all Packt books you have purchased from your account at http://www.packtpub.com. If you purchased this book elsewhere, you can visit http://www.packtpub.com/support and register to have the files e-mailed directly to you.

Microsoft Windows Assessment and Deployment Kit

VMM requires two components of the **Assessment and Deployment Kit** (**ADK**) from Microsoft to be installed:

- ▶ Deployment Tools
- ▶ Windows Pre-installation Environment

The following screenshot shows these two components selected in the installation screen:

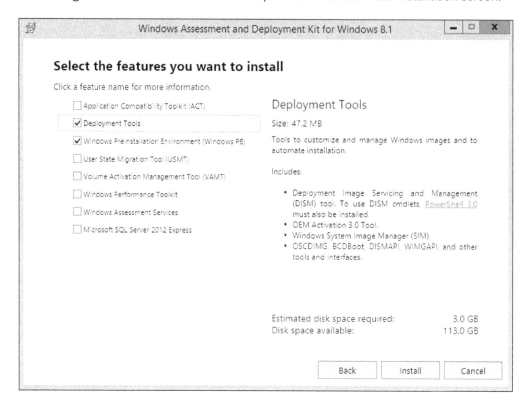

 Please ensure these components are installed prior to installing VMM. You can obtain the ADK from http://www.microsoft.com/en-us/download/details.aspx?id=39982.

SQL Server 2012

VMM requires the following SQL Server 2012 components to be installed:

  ▸ **Database Engine Services**

  ▸ **Management Tools – Complete**

There are no special SQL collation requirements for VMM. When installing SQL Server, it will determine the appropriate collation according to the language of the operating system.

During the installation, the **SVC_VMMSQLAgnt** account was assigned to run the **SQL Agent Service** and the **SVC_VMMSQLEng** account was assigned to run the **SQL Server Service**, as shown in the following screenshot:

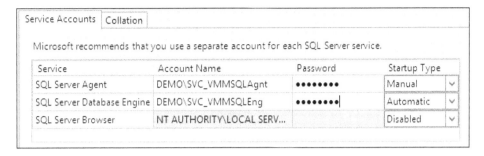

Once SQL Server has been installed, then VMM can be installed.

VMM installation

Ensure the **Install_VMM** and **SVC_VMMSrvc** accounts have been granted administrative rights to the server where VMM will be installed. Additionally, the **Install_VMM** account requires the following permissions in the SQL instance:

▶ The **ALTER ANY LOGIN** permission on the server or membership in the securityadmin fixed server role

▶ The **CREATE DATABASE, CREATE ANY DATABASE**, or **ALTER ANY DATABASE** permissions

Alternatively, the VirtualManagerDB database can be precreated in the SQL instance, in which case the **Install_VMM account** would only require the ALTER ANY LOGIN permission on the server or membership in the securityadmin fixed server role. The VMM Service Account (SVC_VMMSrvc) and the Install_VMM accounts require SQL logins to be created and have the db_owner rights assigned to VirtualManagerDB.

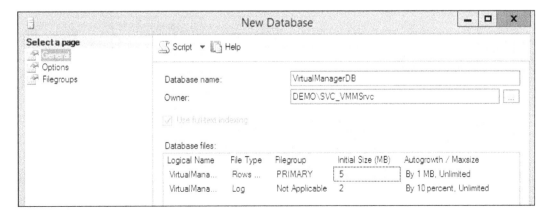

The SVC_VMMSrvc only has the **public** Server role, as shown in the following screenshot:

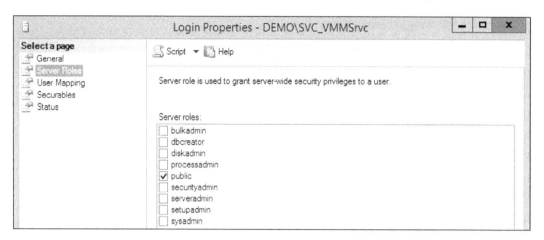

Add the **securityadmin** role to the **Install_VMM** login.

Once the **VirtualManagerDB** database has been created, create a new user in the database for the **Install_VMM** user.

1. Log in to the server where you wish to install VMM with the **Install_VMM account**. Insert or mount the VMM installation media and launch the installation for VMM using the `setup.exe` file. On the installation screen, click on **Install**.

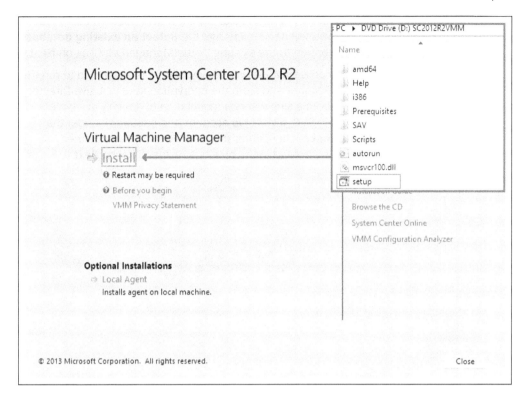

2. When prompted to select which features to install, select **VMM management server** (this will automatically select the **VMM console** option). Click on **Next**.

3. On the **Product registration information** page, enter the appropriate details. If you do not enter a product key, then VMM will be installed in the evaluation mode. It is possible to enter a product key post installation. Click on **Next**.

4. Review the **Please read this license agreement** page and accept to continue with the installation. Click on **Next**.

5. Select whether or not to participate in the **Customer Experience Improvement Program (CEIP)**. Click on **Next**.

6. When prompted whether or not to turn on Microsoft Update, it is suggested *not* to use Microsoft Update. System Center should be updated as per Microsoft guidelines and VMM updates have been known to include SQL scripts that must be executed manually to complete the update. Select **Off** and click on **Next**.

7. On the **Select the installation location** page, accept the default installation location or specify a custom location. Click on **Next**.

8. Provided your machine passes the prerequisite check, which it should if all preceding steps have been followed, you will need to change the **Select an existing database or create a new database** option to the existing VirtualManagerDB. Click on **Next**.

9. While not strictly necessary on a single server deployment, it is suggested to run the VMM Service as a Domain Account and store the encryption keys in Active Directory. This will allow you to move from a single server installation to a highly available installation. Enter the **DEMO\SVC_VMMSrvc** account and password; under the **Distributed Key Management** section, enter the distinguished name of the DKMVMM container that was created in the previous recipe. Click on **Next**.

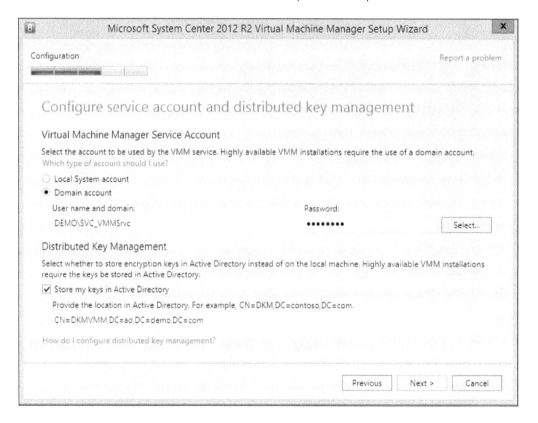

10. Leave the **Port configuration** option as default unless you require different ports. Click on **Next**.

11. On the **Library configuration** page, leave the selections as default. Click on **Next**.

12. Review the **Installation summary** information and click on **Install**.

13. If prompted, follow the instructions for the registration of Service Principle Names in Active Directory. This completes the installation of VMM. You can review the setup logs at `C:\ProgramData\VMMLogs`.

How it works...

Installing VMM on a single server is very simple, and the most important phase is the prerequisites; these must be completed prior to the installation.

The service account specified for the VMM Management Service to use is granted the required permissions on the database during installation, unless you precreated the database.

 While it is possible to install all of the required VMM components on a single server, it is not recommended for a production environment. Hyper-V Network Virtualization with VMM utilizes the VMM management server, and subsequently the database, significantly more than traditional VLAN networking in Hyper-V.

Installing a highly available Virtual Machine Manager server

This recipe provides the steps required to install VMM on a multiserver environment. This will involve creating several Windows Server Failover Clusters:

▸ A cluster of two servers for a SQL Server 2012 AlwaysOn Availability Group

▸ A cluster of two servers for VMM Management Server

▸ A cluster of two servers for the VMM Library Server

A multiserver installation for VMM can give you a great deal of flexibility and resiliency in the overall installation.

Getting ready

You will need three Windows Server Failover Clusters created for this recipe. You will need to create a Computer object in Active Directory for each of the following clustered roles:

▸ SQL Server Availability Group Listener: in this example it will be **SysCtrDBS-AGL**

▸ The name of the VMM Client Access Point; in this example, it will be **VMMMS**

▸ The name of the File Server Client Access Point; in this example, it will be **VMMLibServer**

Please ensure that you have created the computer account objects for SysCtrDBS-AGL, VMMMS, and VMMLibraryServer in Active Directory and granted sufficient privileges to the associated Cluster computer accounts for these objects. Additionally, please ensure that these computer account objects are *disabled* in Active Directory.

How to do it...

The following diagram shows you the high-level steps involved in this recipe and the tasks required to complete this recipe:

Overview of Recipe:

Prerequisites (not covered by this recipe):
- Creation of 3 Windows Server Failover Clusters (only the cluster for VMM Library requires shared storage)
- Creation of the required computer objects in Active Directory for the clustered roles and the associated security settings

Actions:
- Creation of SQL Server AlwaysOn High Availability Group and Listener for use by VMM
- Installation of VMM on a Windows Server Failover Cluster
- Creation of clustered file server role for the VMM Library
- Adding of the clustered file server to VMM to use as the VMM Library

The preceding steps will result in the following VMM components being installed in the following configuration:

- The VirtualManagerDB database will be installed on a new SQL Server 2012 AlwaysOn Availability Group

- VMM 2012 R2 Management Server will be installed on two servers with the System Center Virtual Machine Manager service being a clustered role

- A clustered file server with the VMM Library share deployed

To learn how to install the following components, please visit the following links for Microsoft TechNet:

- Installation of SQL Server ready for AlwaysOn: `http://technet.microsoft.com/en-us/library/bb500395(v=sql.110).aspx`

- Configuration of the Windows Firewall to permit the required network traffic: `http://technet.microsoft.com/en-gb/library/cc753558.aspx`

- Creating Computer Accounts in Active Directory: `http://technet.microsoft.com/en-us/library/cc781364(v=ws.10).aspx`

SQL Server

The first step is to create the SQL Server 2012 AlwaysOn Availability Group (this is a feature of SQL Server Enterprise Edition) for VMM to be installed against. It is assumed that you have installed SQL Server 2012 SP1 on both of your cluster nodes, but have not created the AlwaysOn Availability Group and the associated Listener. Now, you need to perform the following steps:

1. On the first SQL node, for this example **DEMO-SQL01**, open the **SQL Server Configuration Manager** application, right-click on the SQL Server Service instance under **SQL Server Services** and click on **Properties**. On the **AlwaysOn High Availability** tab, check the **Enable AlwaysOn Availability Groups** checkbox. Then, restart the SQL Server service after enabling this checkbox.

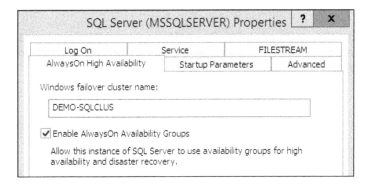

2. Perform the same task on the second SQL Server node.

3. On the first SQL node, open SQL Server Management Studio and create a database called `TmpVMMDB`. A database is required to create the AlwaysOn Availability Group against. Once VMM has been installed, the database can be removed.

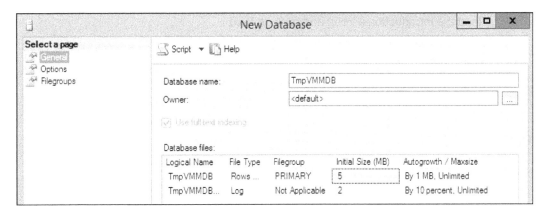

4. Ensure the **Recovery Model** dropdown of the database is set to **Full**. Perform a full backup of the TmpVMMDB database. If you do not do this, you will not be able to create the Availability Group.

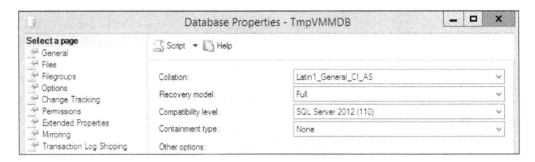

5. On the first SQL node, open SQL Server Management Studio, expand the **AlwaysOn High Availability** folder, right-click on **Availability Groups**, and select **New Availability Group Wizard**, as shown in the following screenshot:

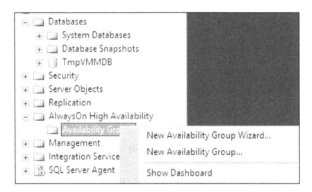

6. Read the introduction screen and click on **Next**.

7. Provide a name of the Availability Group; in this example, it will be SysCtrDBs. Click on **Next**.

8. Select the **TmpVMMDB** database to be added to the Availability Group. Click on **Next**.

9. On the **Specify Replicas** page, click on **Add Replica** and enter the name of the other SQL node. Click on **Connect**.

10. Once the server has been added, set the options as shown in the following screenshot:

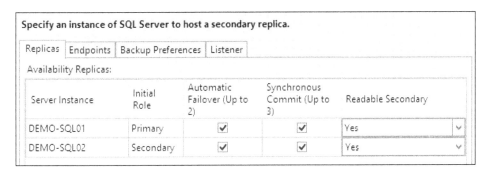

11. Click on the **Listener** tab and select the option to **Create an availability group listener**. In this example, it will be called `SysCtrDBs-AGL`. It will listen on port `1433` and have a static IP address. Once configured, click on **Next**.

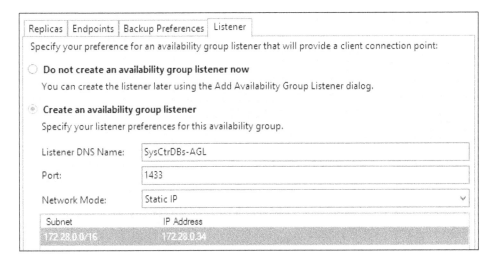

12. On the **Select Initial Data Synchronization** page, enter a file share that the account the SQL Server Agent service is running under has **Full** control over. Click on **Next**.

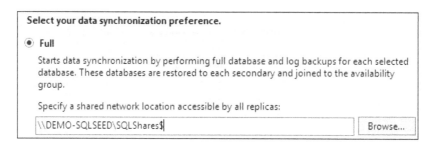

13. The next screen will validate the settings you have entered to ensure the Availability Group can be created. Click on **Next**.

14. After the Availability Group is created, you will have a DNS entry for **SysCtrDBs-AGL** and under **Failover Cluster Manager**, you will see **Role**.

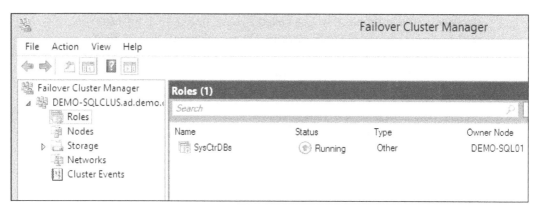

You can then install VMM using the AlwaysOn Availability Group listener name as the name of the SQL Server.

VMM Management Server

When you install VMM, the installation process can detect if it is running on a Windows Server Failover Cluster and will install itself as a clustered role. There is very little difference in the installation process from installing VMM on a standalone server. However, it must be noted that the System Center Virtual Machine Manager service *must* run under a domain account and that the Distributed Key Management container must be created in Active Directory and configured for use during installation. The **svc_VMMSrvc** account must be a member of the Local Administrators group on the server.

As an alternative to precreating the database as we did in the previous recipe, you could make sure the **Install_VMM** account has **sysadmin** privileges on the SQL Server instance.

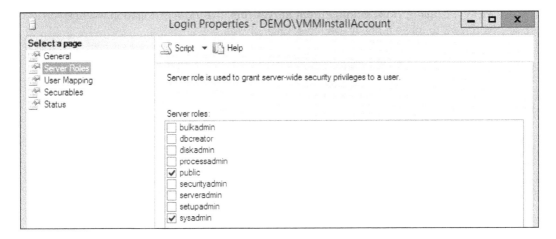

Installing of the first cluster node

As seen in the following screenshot, the cluster has been created; however, there are no roles on the cluster:

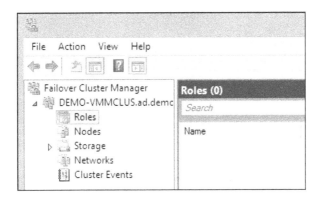

The installation process of VMM is very similar to installing VMM on a single server; however, there are few differences. The steps for installation are as follows:

1. When installing **VMM management server role**, the VMM installation will ask you if you want to make it highly available. Click on **Yes**.

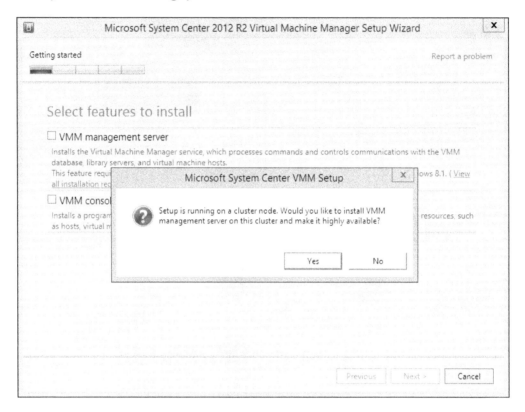

2. When selecting the SQL Server to use for the installation of VirtualManagerDB, you must select **SQL Server AlwaysOn High Availability Group Listener**.

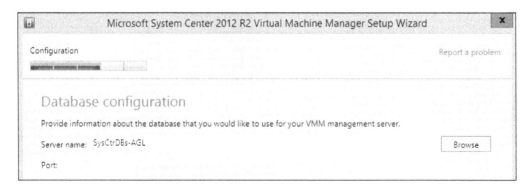

3. You will be prompted to enter the name of the **Client Access Point** for the VMM instance and the IP address you want to assign, which is VMMMS in this case.

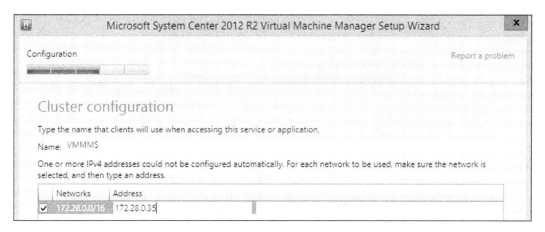

4. When installing VMM on a failover cluster, you will *not* be able to create a library share on the server.

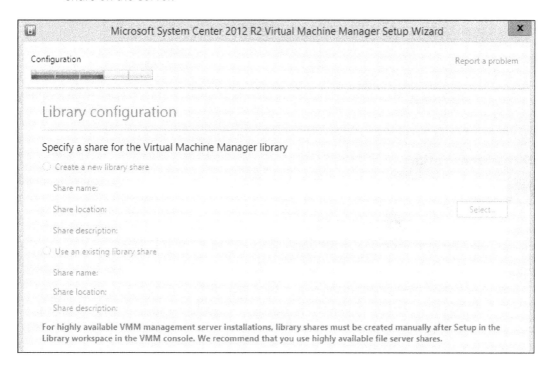

5. After the installation is complete, the **VMMMS** role can be seen in **Failover Cluster Manager**, as shown in the following screenshot:

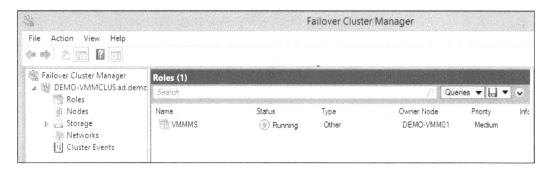

6. If you examine the **VMMMS** role, you can see that only one node can possibly own the role at the moment.

SQL Server tasks

Once the first VMM installation is complete, there are a number of SQL Server tasks that need to be performed:

1. Add the **SVC_VMMSrvc** SQL Login to the other SQL Server node.

2. Alter the recovery model of the **VirtualManagerDB** database to **Full**.

3. Create a full backup of **VirtualManagerDB**.

4. Add **VirtualManagerDB** to the AlwaysOn High Availability Group.

5. Remove **TmpVMMDB** from the AlwaysOn High Availability Group.

Adding SVC_VMMSrvc SQL Login to the other SQL Server node

The SQL Server Logins that have been created by the VMM installation process must be created in every other node of the SQL Server AlwaysOn High Availability Group. Failure to complete this will result in VMM inability to access the database should it failover. This is because unlike Failover Clustering, which protects the entire SQL Server instance, SQL Server AlwaysOn High Availability Groups only protect databases.

1. As shown in the following screenshot, the **SVC_VMMSrvc** Login is not present on the second SQL Server node in the AlwaysOn High Availability Group, **DEMO-SQL02**:

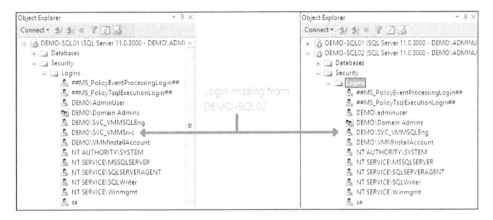

2. Add the SQL Login for the **SVC_VMMSrvc** account by executing the following T-SQL in SQL Server Management Studio:

```
CREATE LOGIN [DEMO\SVC_VMMSrvc] FROM WINDOWS
GO
```

Altering the recovery model of the VirtualManagerDB database to Full

All databases that are to be included in a SQL Server AlwaysOn High Availability Group must use the Full recovery model.

To alter the recovery model, open the first SQL Server node in **SQL Server Management Studio**, right-click on the database, and click on **Properties**. In the **Select a page** section, click on **Options** and change the **Recovery model** to **Full**, as shown in the following screenshot:

Creating a full backup of VirtualManagerDB

In SQL Server Management Studio, perform a full backup of the VirtualManagerDB database.

Adding VirtualManagerDB to AlwaysOn High Availability Group

To add VirtualManagerDB to the AlwaysOn High Availability Group, perform the following steps:

1. Open SQL Server Management Studio, navigate to **AlwaysOn High Availability | SysCtrDBs (Primary)**, right-click on **Availability Databases**, and click on **Add Database**. This is shown in the following screenshot:

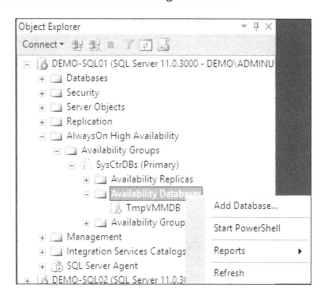

2. Read the introduction screen and click on **Next**.

3. Select **VirtualManagerDB**, ensure the database has "Meets requirements". If not, ensure you have changed the **Recovery model** option to **Full** and created a full backup. Click on **Next**.

4. On the **Select Initial Data Synchronization** page, the share that was previously used will be shown. Change this share if necessary. Click on **Next**.

5. You will then be prompted to connect to the second node of the AlwaysOn High Availability Group. Click on **Connect**. Then, click on **Connect** again. Click on **Next**.

6. Ensure the validation checks are all passed; if not, rectify the failures. Click on **Next**.

7. On the **Summary** page, click on **Finish**.

The VirtualManagerDB database will then be added to the AlwaysOn High Availability Group.

Removing TmpVMMDB from AlwaysOn High Availability Group

Now that the VirtualManagerDB database has been added to the AlwaysOn High Availability Group, the TmpVMMDB database can be removed from the SysCtrDBs AlwaysOn High Availability Group. To do this, perform the following steps:

1. Open SQL Server Management Studio, navigate to **AlwaysOn High Availability** | **SysCtrDBs (Primary)** | **Availability Databases,** right-click on **TmpVMMDB**, and click on **Remove Database from Availability Group**. This is shown in the following screenshot:

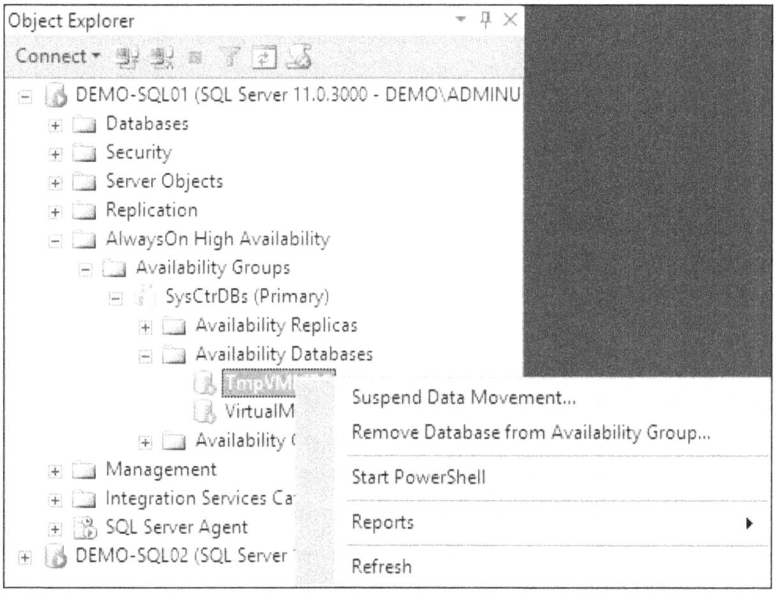

2. In the **Remove Database from Availability Group 'SysCtrDBs'** screen, click on **OK**.
3. The copies of **TmpVMMDB** can then be deleted from each of the SQL Servers.

Installing the second node

The SVC_VMMSrvc account must be a member of the Local Administrators group on the server. You need to perform the following steps for this:

1. When selecting to install the VMM Management Server role, the VMM installation will ask you to add this server to the already highly available installation. Click on **Yes**.

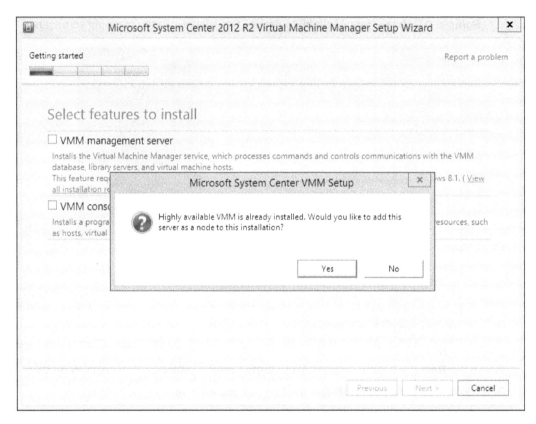

2. During the installation of VMM, there are few decisions to be made. When prompted to choose the SQL Server, all the options are grayed out as shown in the following screenshot:

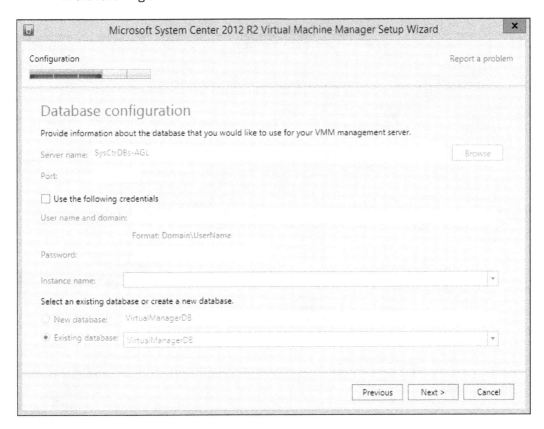

3. On the next screen, the options are grayed out as these are controlled by the cluster and the Distributed Key Management information has already been populated. However, you *must* enter the password for the service account as shown in the following screenshot:

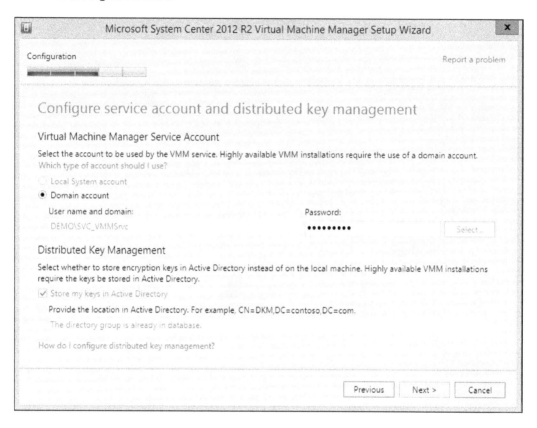

4. After the installation completes, if you investigate the VMMMS role, you can see that both nodes are now possible owners of the role.

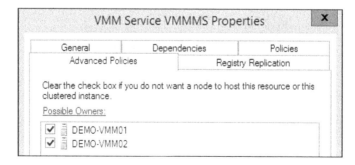

VMM Library Server

The VMM Library Server can use a Clustered File Server that has been created as File Server for general use rather than Scale-Out File Server for application data. To do so, perform the following steps:

1. Open **Failover Cluster Manager** on one of the cluster nodes that will host the VMM Library Server.

2. Right-click on the cluster and click on **Configure Role**.

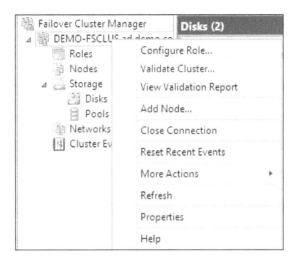

3. Click on **Next.**

4. Click on **File Server**.

5. Click on **Next**.

6. Select **File Server for general use**.

7. Click on **Next**.

8. Enter the name of the **Client Access Point** for the File Server; in this case, VMMLibServer. Then, enter an IP address and click on **Next**.

9. Select the available storage to be assigned to the File Server. Click on **Next**.

10. Click on **Next**.

11. Click on **Finish**.

12. The **VMMLibServer** role can be seen in **Failover Cluster Manager**.

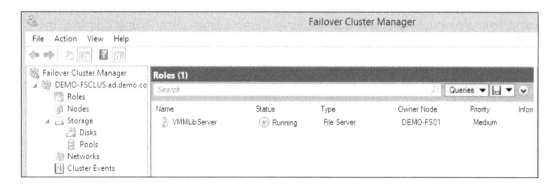

13. To add a share to the File Server, right-click on the **VMMLibServer** role and click on **Add File Share**.

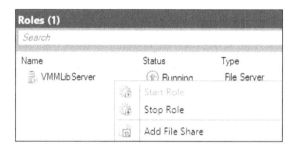

14. In the **File share** profile, select **SMB Share – Quick**. Click on **Next**.

15. Select the appropriate volume. Click on **Next**.

16. Enter a name in the **Share name** field, in this case `Library`. Enter a description for the share, as shown in the following screenshot:

17. Click on **Next**.

18. Uncheck the **Allow caching of share** checkbox. Click on **Next**.

19. The minimum permissions required for a VMM Library share is for the SYSTEM account to have full access in Share Permissions and NTFS Permission. However, as users may need to contribute content to the share, ensure the appropriate users and/or security groups have the appropriate permissions. Click on **Next**.

20. Click on **Create**. This share is ready for use by VMM as a Library Share. You must ensure that the svc_VMMAgntRA account has administrative rights on both nodes of the file server cluster.

Adding a VMM Run As account for the SVC_VMMAgntRA account

Before the Library Server can be added to the VMM, you must create a Run As Account in VMM. This determines the credentials that VMM uses to manage remote systems. Perform the following steps:

1. Open the VMM Console on one of the VMM servers. Remember to connect to VMMMS:8100 as shown in the following screenshot:

2. Navigate to the **Settings** section and click on **Security**. You can see the default **Run As Accounts** created by the VMM installation.

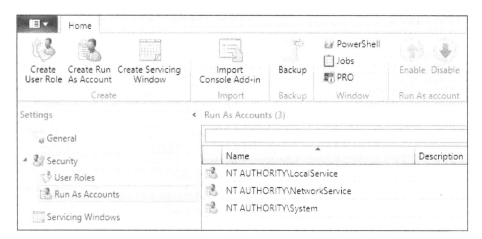

3. Click on **Create Run As Account** on the ribbon bar, enter the details as appropriate, and click on **OK**.

Adding Cluster to VMM

You also need to add Cluster to VMM. For this you need to perform the following steps:

1. Open the VMM console on one of the VMM servers. Remember to connect to VMMMS:8100 as shown in the following screenshot:

2. Navigate to the **Fabric** workspace, expand the **Infrastructure** option, right-click on **Library Servers**, and then click on **Add Library Server**.

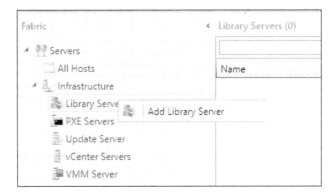

3. Select the **VMM Agent Run As** account, as shown in the following screenshot, and click on **Next**.

4. Enter VMMLibServer in the **Computer name** field and click on **Add**. VMM can then see the clustered role and all the servers that form that role. Click on **Next**.

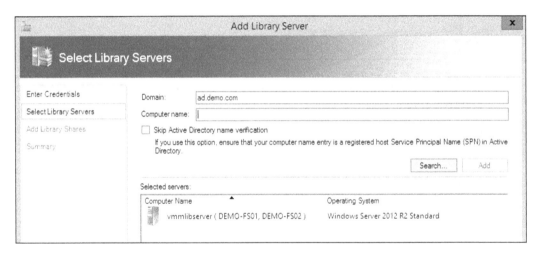

5. Select the **Library** share created previously and check the checkbox under **Add Default Resources**. Click on **Next**.

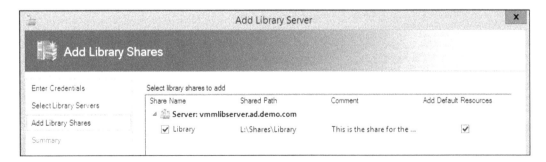

6. Review the summary and click on **Add Library Servers**.

7. Once the VMM job is complete, you will see the two nodes of the File Server cluster and the Client Access Point listed in the **Library Servers** section, as shown in the following screenshot:

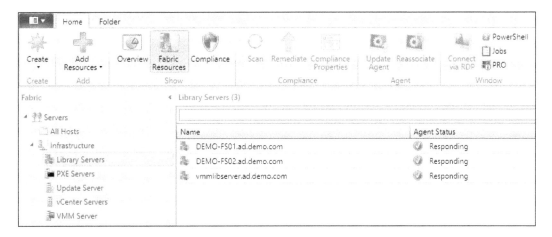

How it works...

While installation of VMM in a highly available configuration can be time consuming, it can help reduce, if not eliminate, the number of single points of failure for the installation.

Through the use of failover clusters (including SQL Server AlwaysOn High Availability Groups), each component can be made highly available. Each role can move from one server in the cluster to another. This allows the VMM service and its required components to remain online while underlying aspects are maintained such as the Windows Server installations.

 As domain user service accounts are used for all services, ensure these accounts are allowed the **Log on as a service** privilege.

2
Configuring Networks for Hyper-V Network Virtualization

In this chapter, we will cover the following recipes:

- ▶ Creating the required Logical Networks in Virtual Machine Manager
- ▶ Creating the required Port Profiles in Virtual Machine Manager
- ▶ Creating and assigning Logical Switches to Hyper-V hosts
- ▶ Creating the Virtual Machine Networks for Tenants
- ▶ Testing the basic Virtual Machine Networks

Introduction

Virtual Machine Manager (**VMM**) uses the concept of Logical Networks to define sites, IP pools, and VLANs. For example, you could create a Logical Network called Host Management; this network would be responsible for managing Hyper-V hosts. You could then create Logical Network Sites within the Logical Network for each data center you have and associate the correct VLAN and subnet details as necessary.

The Hyper-V implementation used in this book will be based on the Converged Network Model. The following diagram shows the design of the Hyper-V Host:

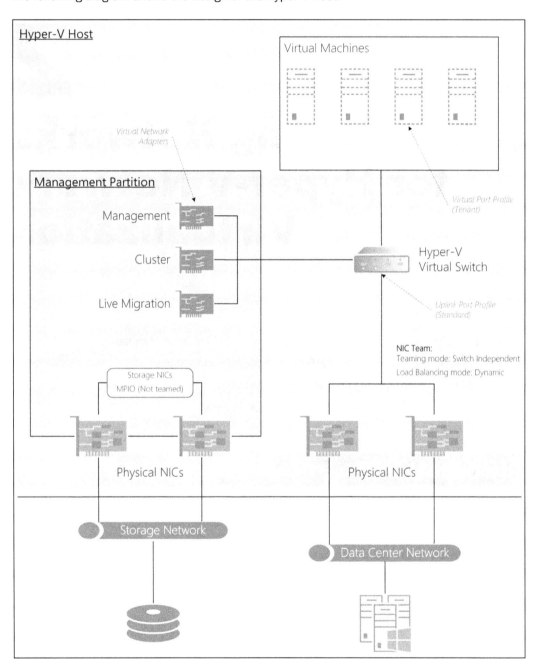

The configuration of the network and the placement of the virtual machines is shown in the following diagram:

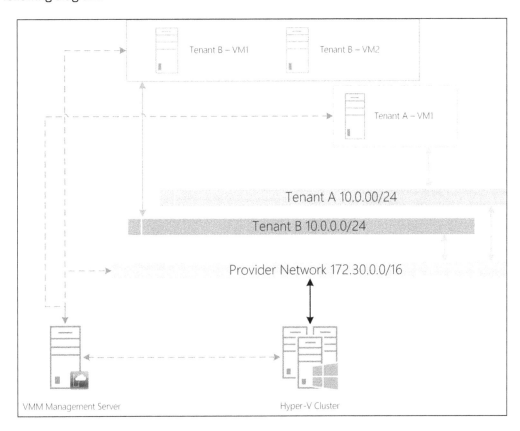

Tenant B – VM1   Tenant B – VM2

Tenant A – VM1

Tenant A 10.0.00/24

Tenant B 10.0.0.0/24

Provider Network 172.30.0.0/16

VMM Management Server   Hyper-V Cluster

Creating the required Logical Networks in Virtual Machine Manager

This recipe provides the steps necessary to create all the required Logical Networks in VMM:

> ▶ **Hyper-V Host Management**: This is used by VMM to communicate with the Hyper-V hosts. For example, when VMM wants a new virtual machine created, it will use this network to communicate with the Hyper-V hosts.

> ▶ **Hyper-V Live Migration**: This is used by Hyper-V for live migration of virtual machines between hosts in a cluster.

> ▶ **Hyper-V Clustering**: This is used by Windows Failover Clustering to maintain the cluster and for the Hyper-V servers to exchange information about the roles within.

> ▶ **Provider Address Space**: This is used by Hyper-V Network Virtualization to host and isolate the tenant networks.

Getting ready

Using the information that you gathered in *Chapter 1, Installing Virtual Machine Manager to Prepare VMM*, you will be able to configure VMM. For this cookbook, the following IP ranges will be in use:

Purpose	Subnet	Maximum number of IP Addresses
Hyper-V Host Management	172.28.0.0/16	65534
Hyper-V Live Migration	172.29.1.0/24	254
Hyper-V Clustering	172.29.2.0/24	254
Provider Address Space	172.30.0.0/16	65534

How to do it...

The following diagram shows you the high-level steps involved in this recipe:

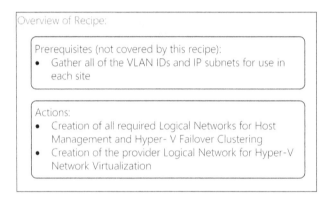

This will result in the creation of the required Logical Networks, Logical Network Sites, and IP Pools. Now, perform the following steps:

1. Open the VMM console and connect to the Management Server. In this case, it will be VMMMS:8100, as shown in the following screenshot:

2. Navigate to **Settings** | **General**, and double-click on **Network Settings**.

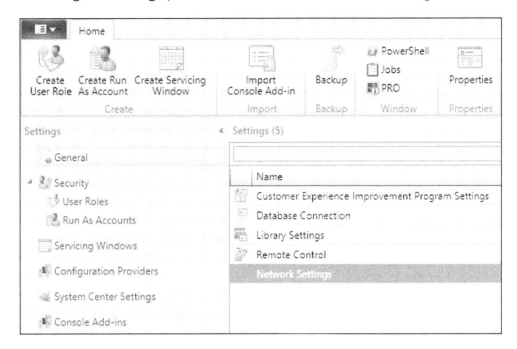

3. Ensure that the **Create logical networks automatically** option is unchecked and click on **OK**.

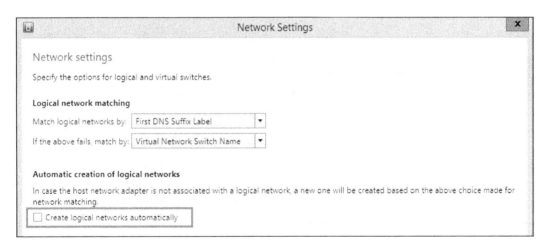

4. Navigate to the **Fabric** section, expand the **Servers** section, right-click on **All Hosts**, and click on **Create Host Group**. Type `Gateway` and press *Enter*. Repeat the process, type `Hosts`, and press *Enter*.

5. Expand the **Networking** option and click on **Logical Networks**. This will currently be empty, as shown in the following screenshot:

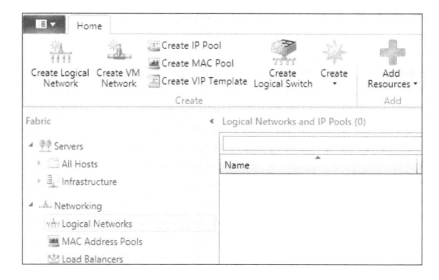

6. On the ribbon bar, click on **Create Logical Network**. This will take you to the **Create Logical Network Wizard** screen. Enter Host-Management in the name, enter an appropriate description, and select the **One connected network** option. Also, ensure that the checkbox for **Create a VM network with the same name to allow virtual machines to access this logical network directly** is ticked (while we will not be connecting VMs to this network, we will be leveraging the converged networking model).

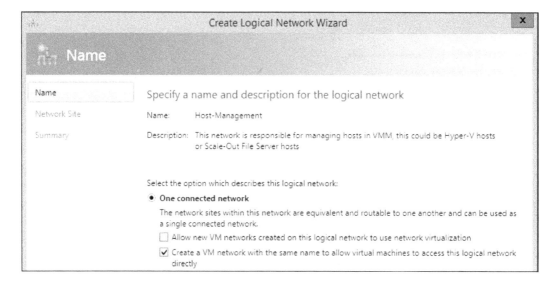

7. On the **Network sites** page (shown in the following screenshot), click on **Add** and select both the newly created host groups, **Gateway** and **Hosts**. For this cookbook, the Host-Management site for both Host Groups will be on **VLAN 0** using **172.28.0.0/16**. Click on **Next**.

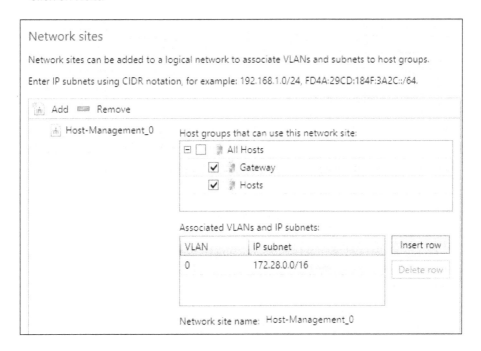

8. On the summary screen, click on the **View Script** button in the top-right corner.

9. This will open a copy of the PowerShell cmdlets that VMM is about to execute:

```
$logicalNetwork = New-SCLogicalNetwork -Name "Host-
  Management" -LogicalNetworkDefinitionIsolation $false -
    EnableNetworkVirtualization $false -UseGRE $false -
      IsPVLAN $false -Description "This network is
        responsible for managing hosts in VMM, this could
          be Hyper-V hosts or Scale-Out File Server hosts"
```

```
$allHostGroups = @()
$allHostGroups += Get-SCVMHostGroup -ID "0dfec42b-061f-
    471c-a0a8-55bcfb39382c"
$allHostGroups += Get-SCVMHostGroup -ID "7a9d41ae-fd5f-
    44ad-ae46-36b2f0b7e2d9"
$allSubnetVlan = @()
$allSubnetVlan += New-SCSubnetVLan -Subnet "172.28.0.0/16"
    -VLanID 0
New-SCLogicalNetworkDefinition -Name "Host-Management_0" -
    LogicalNetwork $logicalNetwork -VMHostGroup
        $allHostGroups -SubnetVlan $allSubnetVlan -
        RunAsynchronously
New-SCVMNetwork -Name "Host-Management" -IsolationType
    "NoIsolation" -LogicalNetwork $logicalNetwork
```

Please note that the GUIDs shown in bold in the previous code will likely be different on your installation.

10. Close the Notepad window and click on **Finish** in the wizard. This will create the Host-Management Logical Network and its site.

11. To create an IP pool for the Host-Management network, right-click on the newly created **Host-Management** Logical Network, and click on the **Create IP Pool** option, as shown in the following screenshot:

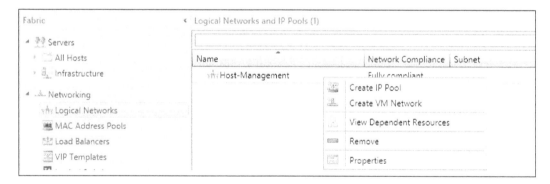

12. Enter a name for the IP pool, in this case Host-Management-IP-Pool, and enter an appropriate description. Click on **Next**.

13. On the next page, ensure that the **Host-Management_0** Logical Network Site is selected, as shown in the following screenshot. Click on **Next**.

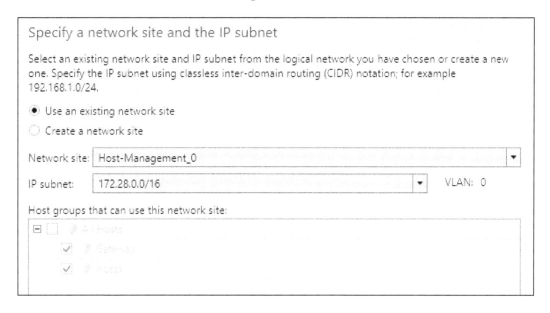

14. Enter the **Starting IP address** and **End IP address** values of the range of IP addresses you would like VMM to distribute. This does not have to be the entire range. To keep consistency between physical networks and Hyper-V Virtual Networks, use the first IP address in the range (.1) as the default gateway; then, set the **Starting IP address** to 172.28.0.2. In this example, the starting IP address is 172.28.0.101 and the end IP address is 172.28.0.250.

If your default gateway is a different IP address, then enter its IP address within the **IP addresses to be reserved for other uses** box if it falls within the range. Click on **Next**.

15. Enter the gateway address(es) for the IP pool and any metric information required. In this example, enter 172.28.0.1, or the gateway address in your network. Click on **Next**.

16. Enter the DNS server address(es) and order them appropriately. Additionally, enter the DNS suffix for the connection and any other DNS search suffixes as required. In this example, enter 172.28.0.4, or the DNS server addresses in your network. Click on **Next**.

17. Enter a WINS server IP address if you have one. There is no WINS server in this example. Click on **Next**.

18. On the summary screen, click on the **View Script** button in the top-right corner. This will open a copy of the PowerShell cmdlets that VMM is about to execute:

```
$logicalNetwork = Get-SCLogicalNetwork -ID "f69abe75-0e94-
    42a9-b86a-6d48c4010c1a"
$logicalNetworkDefinition = Get-SCLogicalNetworkDefinition
    -LogicalNetwork $logicalNetwork -Name "Host-Management_0"

# Gateways
$allGateways = @()
$allGateways += New-SCDefaultGateway -IPAddress
    "172.28.0.1" -Automatic

# DNS servers
$allDnsServer = @("172.28.0.4")

# DNS suffixes
$allDnsSuffixes = @()

# WINS servers
$allWinsServers = @()

New-SCStaticIPAddressPool -Name "Host-Management-IP-Pool" -
    LogicalNetworkDefinition $logicalNetworkDefinition -
        Subnet "172.28.0.0/16" -IPAddressRangeStart
            "172.28.0.101" -IPAddressRangeEnd "172.28.0.250" -
                DefaultGateway $allGateways -DNSServer
                    $allDnsServer -DNSSuffix "ad.demo.com" -
                        DNSSearchSuffix $allDnsSuffixes -
                            RunAsynchronously -Description "This is the
                                set of address that VMM can allocate to
                                    hosts for management purposes"
```

Please note that the GUIDs shown in bold in the previous code will likely be different on your installation.

19. You will then see the IP pool appear under the Logical Network in the VMM console.

Logical Networks and IP Pools (1)

Name	Network Compliance	Subnet	Begin Address	End Address	Available Addresses	Available Addresse...
⊟ ∨Ȧ⋮ Host-Management	Fully compliant					
⛁ Host-Management-IP-Pool	Fully compliant	172.28.0.0/16	172.28.0.101	172.28.0.250	150	150

This process must be repeated for the **Host-Live-Migration** and **Host-Cluster** networks. Alternatively, by leveraging the PowerShell that VMM has already generated for you, it is possible to easily adapt the previous scripts and create the two Logical Networks, the Logical Network sites, and the associated IP pools. The following script shows you what your script could look like:

```
#This file will create the Live Migration and Cluster networks

#region Host-LiveMigration

#Create the Logical Network
$logicalNetwork = New-SCLogicalNetwork -Name "Host-LiveMigration"
  -LogicalNetworkDefinitionIsolation $false -
    EnableNetworkVirtualization $false -UseGRE $false -IsPVLAN
      $false -Description "This network is responsible for Live
        Migration of VMs in Hyper-V"

#Build the Host Groups to assign the Logical Network Site to
$allHostGroups = @()
$allHostGroups += Get-SCVMHostGroup -Name "Gateway"
$allHostGroups += Get-SCVMHostGroup -Name "Hosts"
$allSubnetVlan = @()
$allSubnetVlan += New-SCSubnetVLan -Subnet "172.29.1.0/24" -VLanID
  1000

#Create the Logical Network Site, store in variable for later use
$logicalNetworkDefinition = New-SCLogicalNetworkDefinition -Name
  "Host-LiveMigration_0" -LogicalNetwork $logicalNetwork -
    VMHostGroup $allHostGroups -SubnetVLan $allSubnetVlan

#Create the VM Network so we can use converged networking with
  this network
New-SCVMNetwork -Name "Host-LiveMigration" -IsolationType
  "NoIsolation" -LogicalNetwork $logicalNetwork

#Create IP Pool, very basic as no DNS or Gateways required for
  Live Migration
New-SCStaticIPAddressPool -Name "Host-LiveMigration-IP-Pool" -
  LogicalNetworkDefinition $logicalNetworkDefinition -Subnet
    "172.29.1.0/24" -IPAddressRangeStart "172.29.1.4" -
      IPAddressRangeEnd "172.29.1.254" -Description "This is the
        set of address that VMM can allocate to hosts for Live
          Migration purposes"

#endregion

#region Host-Cluster

#Create the Logical Network
```

```
$logicalNetwork = New-SCLogicalNetwork -Name "Host-Cluster" -
  LogicalNetworkDefinitionIsolation $false -
    EnableNetworkVirtualization $false -UseGRE $false -IsPVLAN
      $false -Description "This network is responsible for cluster
        communications between physical hosts"

#Build the Host Groups to assing the Logical Network Site to
$allHostGroups = @()
$allHostGroups += Get-SCVMHostGroup -Name "Gateway"
$allHostGroups += Get-SCVMHostGroup -Name "Hosts"
$allSubnetVlan = @()
$allSubnetVlan += New-SCSubnetVLan -Subnet "172.29.2.0/24" -VLanID
1001

#Create the Logical Network Site, store in variable for later use
$logicalNetworkDefinition = New-SCLogicalNetworkDefinition -Name
  "Host-Cluster_0" -LogicalNetwork $logicalNetwork -VMHostGroup
    $allHostGroups -SubnetVLan $allSubnetVlan

#Create the VM Network so we can use converged networking with
  this network
New-SCVMNetwork -Name "Host-Cluster" -IsolationType "NoIsolation"
  -LogicalNetwork $logicalNetwork

#Create IP Pool, very basic as no DNS or Gateways required for
  Live Migration
New-SCStaticIPAddressPool -Name "Host-Cluster-IP-Pool" -
  LogicalNetworkDefinition $logicalNetworkDefinition -Subnet
    "172.29.2.0/24" -IPAddressRangeStart "172.29.2.4" -
      IPAddressRangeEnd "172.29.2.254" -Description "This is the
        set of address that VMM can allocate to hosts for cluster
          purposes"

#endregion
```

20. Save the PowerShell file in a location accessible from the VMM server.

21. In the VMM console, click on the **Home** tab in the ribbon bar and then click on the **PowerShell** button. This will launch PowerShell with the VMM module already loaded and the console connected to the current VMM instance. In the PowerShell console, execute the script file saved previously. Once the execution is complete, you will have two new Logical Networks, each with their own Logical Network Site and their own IP pools, as shown in the following screenshot:

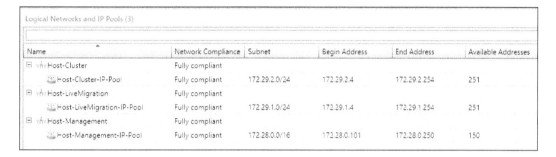

Logical Networks and IP Pools (3)

Name	Network Compliance	Subnet	Begin Address	End Address	Available Addresses
⊟ Host-Cluster	Fully compliant				
Host-Cluster-IP-Pool	Fully compliant	172.29.2.0/24	172.29.2.4	172.29.2.254	251
⊟ Host-LiveMigration	Fully compliant				
Host-LiveMigration-IP-Pool	Fully compliant	172.29.1.0/24	172.29.1.4	172.29.1.254	251
⊟ Host-Management	Fully compliant				
Host-Management-IP-Pool	Fully compliant	172.28.0.0/16	172.28.0.101	172.28.0.250	150

22. Navigate to the **Fabric** section and expand the **Networking** section. To create the **Provider Address** Logical Network, click on the **Create Logical Network** option on the ribbon bar.

23. In the wizard, enter an appropriate name for the Logical Network; in this example, it is `Provider Address`. Ensure that the **One connected network** option is selected and the **Allow new VM networks created on this logical network to use network virtualization** option is checked. Click on **Next**.

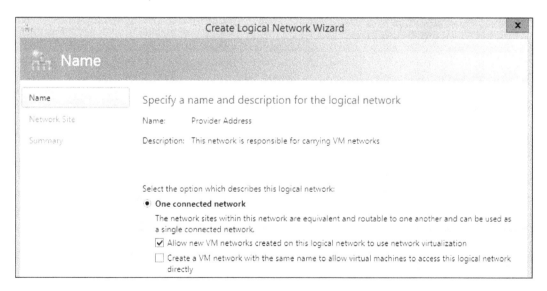

24. Click on **Add** to create a new Network Site that has both the host groups selected, a VLAN ID of **1010**, and subnet of **172.30.0.0/16**.

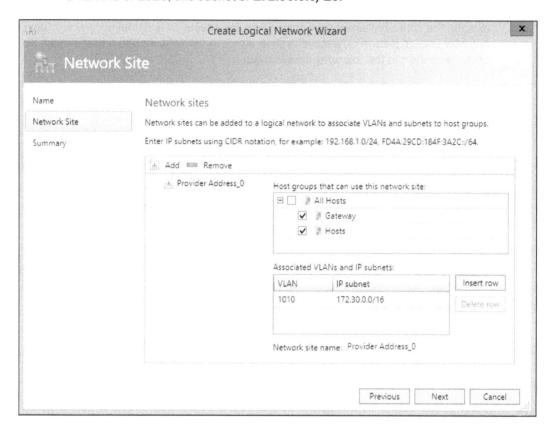

25. Review the summary and click on **Finish**.

This finishes the definition of the current Logical Network requirements.

How it works...

Each Logical Network within VMM represents a purpose; a Logical Network Site tells VMM what VLAN IDs and subnets are associated with that site for each Host Group. This ensures that when VMM needs to allocate an IP address from an associated IP pool or Logical Network Site has been associated in Uplink Port Profile, VMM has terms of reference to use.

This abstracts the information about your network so that VMM can understand it and ensure that when it performs tasks such as creating a virtual machine, the requested network(s) will be available, and if not, it can inform the user.

Creating the required Port Profiles in Virtual Machine Manager

This recipe provides the steps necessary to create all the required Port Profiles in VMM, which are as follows:

- ▸ Uplink Port Profiles that are used for the physical definition of the Logical Switch and deployed to the Hyper-V hosts
- ▸ Virtual Port Profiles that are used to define what types of virtual port are available on the Logical Switch

Getting ready

This recipe requires that you have completed the previous recipe.

How to do it...

The following diagram shows you the high-level steps involved in this recipe:

Overview of Recipe:

Actions:
- Creation of the Virtual Port Profile for use by all HNV tenants
- Creation of the Uplink Port Profile for use by the Hyper-V hosts
- Creation of the Tenant Port Classification

This will result in assigning of the newly created Logical Networks and Sites to a profile that can be applied to the Logical Switch.

1. Open the **Fabric** workspace, expand the **Networking** section, and click on **Port Profiles**. You will see the default Port Profiles that are shipped with VMM, as shown in the following screenshot:

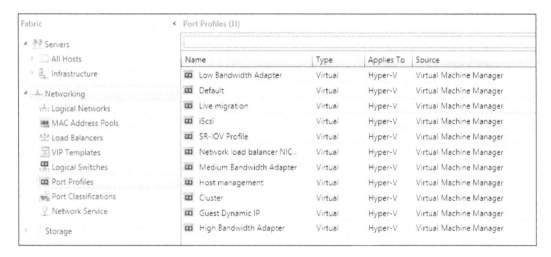

2. Right-click on **Port Profiles**, click on **Create Hyper-V Port Profile**, and select **Virtual network adapter port profile**. Enter an appropriate name, in this case `Tenant`, and a description. Click on **Next**.

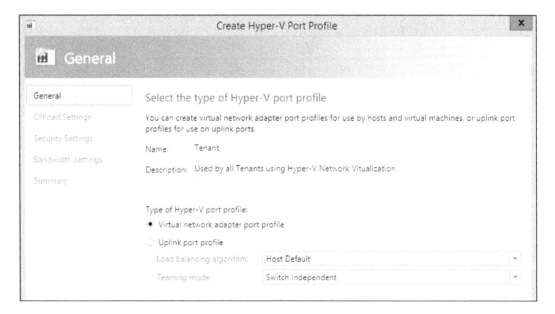

3. On the **Offload Settings** page, ensure that all the settings are *not* selected. Using Hyper-V Network Virtualization will typically break most offloads unless your physical network cards support **NVGRE Task Offload** (please consult your network card manufacturer). Click on **Next**.

4. Accept the defaults on the **Security Settings** page. Click on **Next.**

5. In the **Bandwidth Settings** page (shown in the following screenshot), set **Minimum bandwidth weight** to **1**. Click on **Next**.

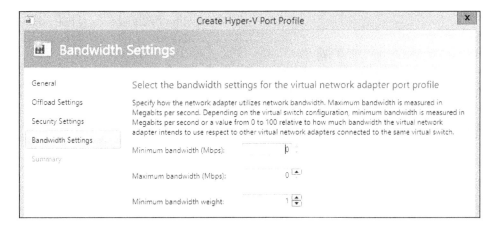

6. Review the **Summary** page and click on **Finish**.

7. Right-click on **Port Profiles** and click on **Create Hyper-V Port Profile**. In the page shown in the following screenshot, select **Uplink port profile**. Enter an appropriate name, in this case `Standard`, and a description. Leave the **Load balancing algorithm** option set to **Host Default** and the **Teaming mode** option set to **Switch Independent**. Click on **Next**.

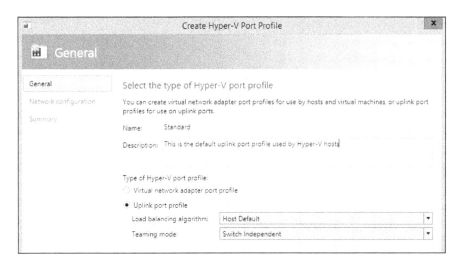

> The Host Default load balancing algorithm on Windows Server 2012 R2 is Dynamic, and it is Hyper-V Port in Windows Server 2012. As Windows Server 2012 R2 is in use, the Uplink Port Profile will automatically use the Dynamic load balancing algorithm by keeping it to Host Default. This Uplink Port Profile could be used with Windows Server 2012 servers.

8. On the **Network Configuration** page, select *all* Logical Network Sites that have been created so far. Check the box **Enable Hyper-V Network Virtualization** (while not strictly necessary for Windows Server 2012 R2, it is a good practice in case this uplink port profile gets applied to a Windows Server 2012 Hyper-V host). Click on **Next**.

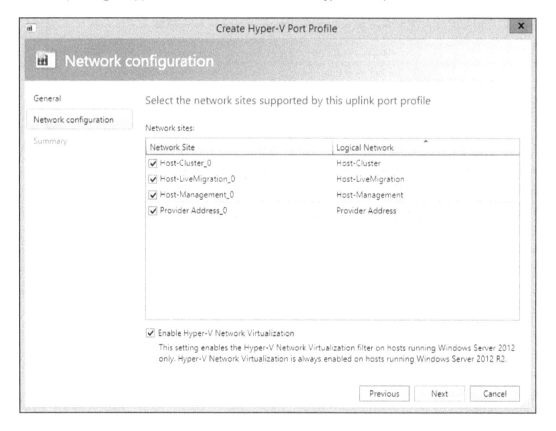

9. Review the **Summary** page and click on **Finish**.

10. Navigate to **Fabric | Networking**, right-click on **Port Classifications**, and click on **Create Port Classification**.

11. Enter a name for port classification, in this case `Tenant`, and enter a description as shown in the following screenshot:

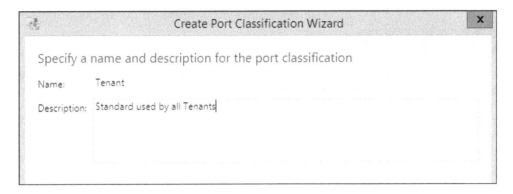

12. Click on **OK.**

How it works...

Uplink Port Profiles is what VMM uses to control what Logical Network Sites, and therefore what Logical Networks, are available in any given location. This relates to the physical adapters. For example, if VLAN IDs 10, 20 and 30 are available, then VMM will not allow a virtual machine with a VLAN ID of 40 to be deployed to a Logical Switch with that uplink port profile. Virtual Port Profiles control the characteristics of a virtual machine's network adapter.

When these two items are combined on a Logical Switch, it controls the details given to a virtual machine's network adapter. For example, if a VM is requesting to be connected to a specific network, then VMM knows the VLAN ID, if appropriate, and the subnet of that network in the required location. This allows VMM to ensure that the network adapter has the correct options configured.

Creating and assigning Logical Switches to Hyper-V hosts

Now that the Logical Networks and Uplink and Virtual Port Profiles have been created, they need to be applied to a Logical Switch.

As the converged networking model will be used, the Logical Switch will have several virtual NICs created for the Management OS to use:

▶ Management
▶ Live Migration
▶ Cluster

You will need to have a Hyper-V cluster with no logical switches (or standard switches) configured and attached to VMM. Please visit `http://technet.microsoft.com/en-gb/library/gg610621.aspx` for details.

Getting ready

As a prerequisite, all of the previous recipes must be complete. Additionally, you must have at least one Hyper-V host in the environment to test with. Please see `http://technet.microsoft.com/en-us/library/gg610646.aspx` for details on how to add Hyper-V hosts to VMM.

How to do it...

The following diagram shows you the high-level steps involved in this recipe:

Overview of Recipe:

Actions:
- Creation of the "Default" Logical Switch for all Hyper-V hosts
- Deployment the "Default" Logical Switch to all Hyper-V hosts
- Creation of the virtual NIC interfaces on the "Default" Logical Switch for Hyper-V Management, Clustering and Live Migration

This will result in a Logical Switch that is capable of hosting virtual machines using Hyper-V networking virtualization and having a copy of this switch deployed to each Hyper-V host.

The first part of this recipe is to create the Logical Switch. For this, you need to perform the following steps:

1. Navigate to **Fabric | Networking | Logical Switches**, as shown in the following screenshot:

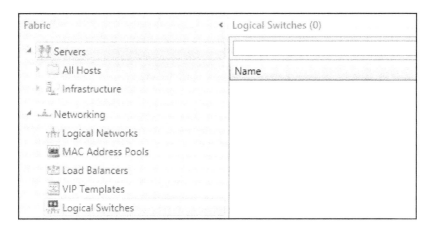

2. Right-click on **Logical Switches** and click on **Create Logical Switch**. Read the introduction and click on **Next**.

3. Enter a name and a description for the Logical Switch. In this case, enter `Default`. Ensure that the **Enable single root I/O virtualization (SR-IOV)** option is *not* checked. Click on **Next**.

4. On the **Extensions** page, leave the default options selected and click on **Next**.

5. On the **Uplink** page, set the **Uplink mode** dropdown to **Team**.

6. To add the Standard Uplink Port Profile, click on **Add**. Select **Standard** from the drop-down list, as shown in the following screenshot. Click on **OK**.

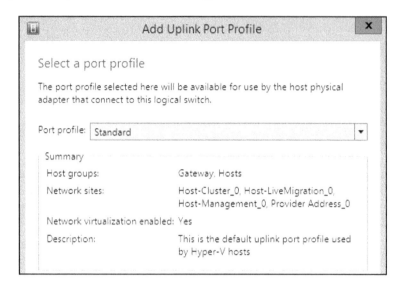

7. Click on **Next**.

8. On the **Virtual Port** page of the wizard, each of the following Virtual Port Profiles have to be added:

   ❏ Host management

   ❏ Live Migration Workload

   ❏ Host Cluster Workload

   ❏ Tenant

To add a Virtual Port Profile, click on **Add**. In the dialog window, select the Port classification from the dropdown, check the box **Include a virtual network adapter port profile in this virtual port**, and ensure that the same name is selected.

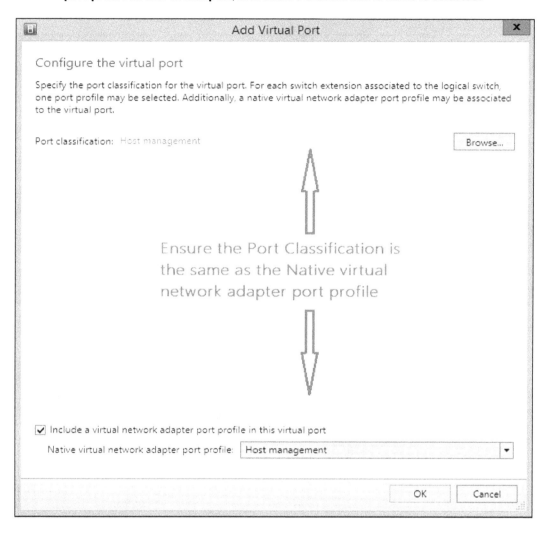

9. Click on **OK** and repeat this process for the other required Virtual Port Profiles. Click on **Tenant** and then click on **Set Default**. This ensures that any network adapter that is attached to this switch that does not have a port classification will be set to use the Tenant profile.

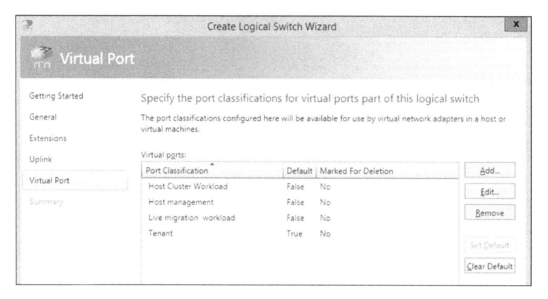

10. Click on **Next**, review the summary, and click on **Finish**.

    The second part of this recipe will be to add the Logical Switches to the Hyper-V hosts.

11. In the **Fabric** workspace, navigate to **Servers | All Hosts | Hosts**. This will show you the Hyper-V hosts in that Host Group; in this example, it is **hypvch1.ad.demo.com** and **hypvch2.ad.demo.com**, as shown in the following screenshot:

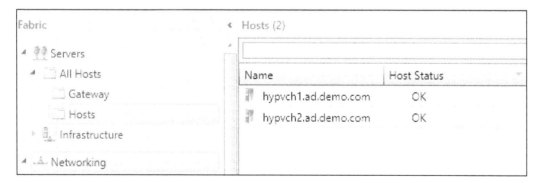

12. Right-click on one of the servers and click on **Properties**. In the **Properties** dialog, click on **Virtual Switches**.

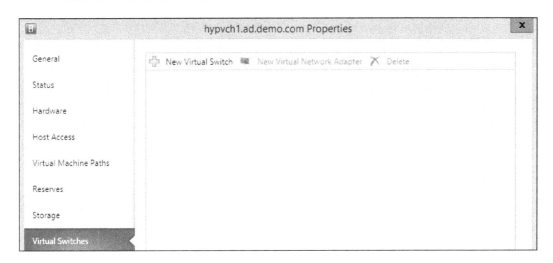

13. Navigate to **New Virtual Switch | New Logical Switch**. As only one Logical Switch is available and one Uplink Port Profile has been attached to the switch, it will select the **Default** Logical Switch and the **Standard** Uplink Port Profile, as shown in the following screenshot:

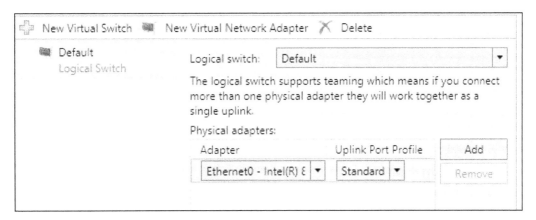

14. Click on **Add** to include all additional NICs that can be included in the NIC Team. In this case, they are **Ethernet0** and **Ethernet1**.

15. Ensure that the **Default Logical Switch** menu is selected on the left and click **New Virtual Network Adapter**. Enter Management as the name, ensure that the **This virtual network adapter inherits settings from the physical management adapter** checkbox is ticked. Ticking this box gives the MAC address of the first physical adapter to this Management Virtual Network adapter and its IP address.

Set the **VM Network** field to **Host-Management** and ensure that under **Port profile**, the **Classification** option is set to **Host management**.

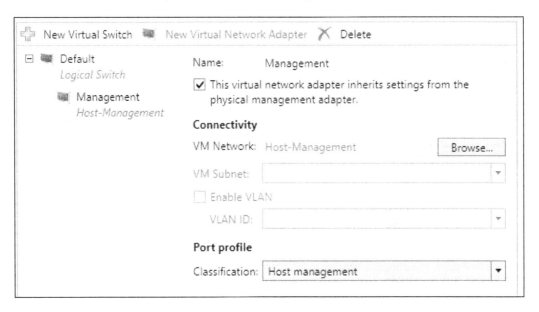

16. Click on the **Default Logical Switch** and then click on **New Virtual Network Adapter** again.

17. Enter Cluster in the name box, ensure that the **This virtual network adapter inherits settings from the physical management adapter** checkbox is *not* ticked.

18. Select the **Host-Cluster** VM Network.

19. Ensure the **VLAN ID** is set correctly; in this example, it should be **1001**.

20. Set the **Port profile** option to **Host Cluster Workload**.

21. Set the **IP address configuration** field to **Static**, as shown in the following screenshot, and select the **Host-Cluster-IP-Pool** option under **IPv4 pool**. You do not need to enter an IP address in the **IPv4 address** box, VMM will automatically assign the next available IP address from the IP pool.

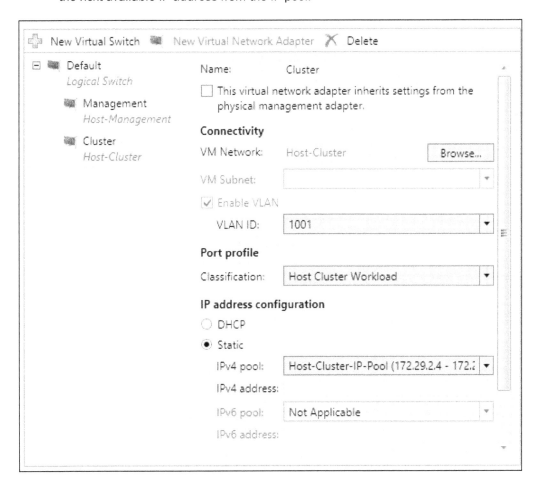

22. Click on **Default Logical Switch** and then click on **New Virtual Network Adapter** again.

23. Enter Live Migration in the name box and ensure that the **This virtual network adapter inherits settings from the physical management adapter** checkbox is *not* ticked.

24. Select the **Host-LiveMigration** VM Network.

25. Ensure that **VLAN** is set correctly, in this case **1000**.

26. Set the Port Profile to **Live migration workload**.

27. Set the IP address configuration to **Static** and select **Host-LiveMigration-IP-Pool** under **IPv4 pool**. You do not need to enter an IP address in the **IPv4 address** box; VMM will automatically assign the next available IP address from the IP pool.

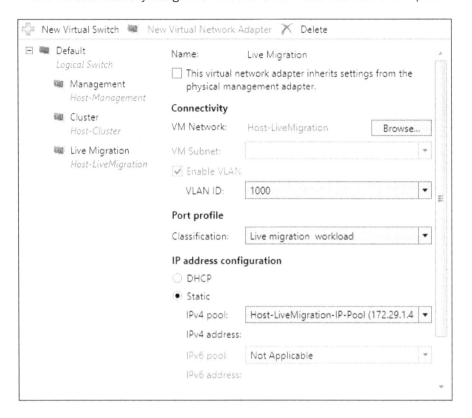

28. Click on **OK**. You will receive a message from VMM warning you that VMM may lose connectivity during configuration of the Networking. Click on **OK**.

29. Once the process is complete, repeat it for all other Hyper-V hosts in the cluster. If you have many hosts, you could look to use PowerShell to make this task faster.

How it works...

The Logical Switch, *Default*, sits on top of the NIC team that was declared in the Standard Uplink Port Profile. The virtual network adapters are then created within the management partition of the Hyper-V host and attached to this Logical Switch; all network traffic from virtual machines and from the host flows through the switch. The weighting that was declared in the tenant Virtual Port Profile and the profiles that were used for the Management, Cluster, and Live Migration ensure that the critical management functions of the Hyper-V host are not overwhelmed by the virtual machine traffic.

There's more...

Now, the Hyper-V hosts have the switches and the required virtual network adapters, so these Hyper-V hosts should be clustered. Please visit `http://technet.microsoft.com/en-gb/library/gg610621.aspx` for instructions on how to cluster these Hyper-V hosts.

Creating the Virtual Machine Networks for Tenants

Each Tenant requires its own VM Network, and optionally a subnet (or several) within. Once the VM Networks for the Tenants have been created, it will be possible to create VMs and deploy them into each VM Network.

A VM Network is the software defined network. Each VM network is completely isolated and you can have up to 16,777,216 VM Networks.

In this recipe, we will create two VM Networks:

- ▸ Tenant A using an IP subnet 10.0.0.0/24
- ▸ Tenant B using an IP subnet 10.0.0.0/24

Getting ready

Decide what VM Network names the Tenants will have and the IP subnets they will have.

How to do it...

The following diagram shows you the high-level steps involved in this recipe:

Overview of Recipe:

Actions:
- Creation of 2 VM Networks (one for Tenant A and one for Tenant B)
- Creation of 1 IP Pool per VM Network

This will result in two VM Networks, each with one IPv4 subnet containing a pool of IPs that can be distributed to newly created VMs. Now perform the following steps:

1. Open the **VMs and Services** workspace, navigate to **VM Networks**. Here, all of the currently created VM Networks will be listed, as shown in the following screenshot:

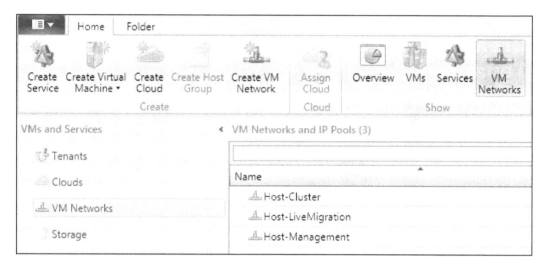

2. Right-click on **VM Networks** and click on **Create VM Network**.

3. Enter a name and an appropriate description for the VM Network; in this example, it will be **Tenant A**. Ensure that Logical Network is set to **Provider Address**. Click on **Next**.

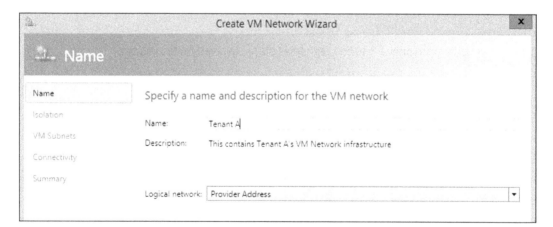

4. When the **Provider Address** Logical Network was created, the option to allow **Hyper-V network virtualization** was checked, and the **Isolation** options within the **Create VM Network Wizard** reflect this. Ensure that **IPv4** is selected for both isolation options. Click on **Next**.

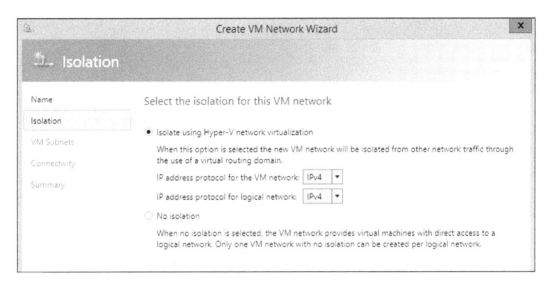

5. Add a single VM subnet in the dialog window. For this example, the subnet name is **Subnet 1** and the subnet is **10.0.0.0/24**. Click on **Next**.

6. You will be notified that no network service that specified a gateway has been added to VMM. This is *not* unexpected. Click on **Next**.

7. Review the summary. You can click the **View Script** to see the PowerShell cmdlets that VMM is about to execute. Click on **Finish**.

8. Repeat steps 2-7, substituting **Tenant B** for **Tenant A**. All other options should remain the same, *including* the subnet details.

9. After you have created the two required VM Networks, you must create an IP Pool for each VM Network. To begin, right-click on the VM Network **Tenant A** and click on **Create IP Pool**.

10. Enter a name and description for the IP; in this case, it is `Subnet 1 - IP Poolpool`. Click on **Next**.

11. On the **IP address range** page, you will see that the range starts automatically at **10.0.0.2**. The first IP address of the subnet is reserved for use by the Hyper-V Network Virtualization gateway and is the default gateway for the subnet. Click on **Next**.

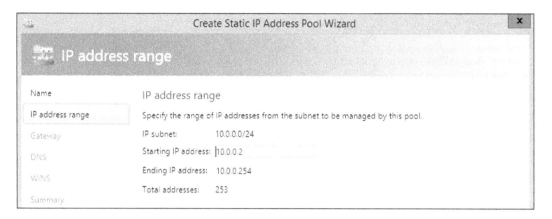

12. Leave the **Gateway** information blank. Click on **Next**.

13. You can enter the IP address for a DNS server that the VMs on this subnet should use. However, as there are no VMs in the subnet and currently no external communication available leave this blank. Click on **Next**.

14. Leave the WINS server blank. Click on **Next**.

15. Review the summary. You can click on the **View Script** to see the PowerShell cmdlets that VMM is about to execute. Click on **Finish**.

16. Repeat steps 9-15 for the **Tenant B** VM Network.

How it works...

The VM Networks are where the Tenant networks are declared, along with its subnets if required. Each VM Network is isolated from one another through the NVGRE protocol, which allows each VM Network to have the same subnets while being isolated.

Testing the basic Virtual Machine Networks

Now that all of the building blocks are in place, it is time to deploy two VMs—one into Tenant A's VM Network and one into Tenant B's VM Network. Once this is complete, another VM will be deployed for further testing.

The following diagram shows how the VMs will be connected to the network:

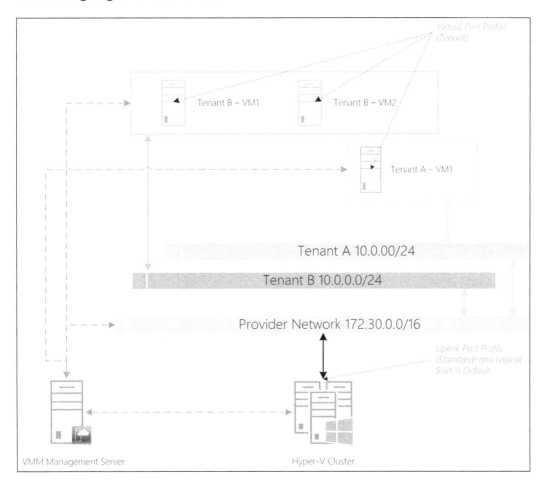

Getting ready

You will need to have a VM Template set up that is not connected to any VM Network in the template, this can then be assigned during deployment.

Please visit `http://technet.microsoft.com/en-gb/library/hh427282.aspx` for information on how to create a VM template.

The operating system used for all VMs in this cookbook is Windows Server 2012 R2 Standard with a GUI and they only have a single Network Adapter. Please see *Appendix, VM Templates*, for detailed information on the VM template used.

How to do it...

The following diagram shows you the high-level steps involved in this recipe:

Overview of Recipe:

Actions:
- Creation of 2 VMs, one in each VM Network
- Prove that each VM is isolated
- Deploy another VM with a matching IP address but in a different VM Network

This will result in three VMs deployed, two in one VM Network and one in the other. You will be able to prove that they are isolated from one another. Now, you have to perform the following steps:

1. Navigate to the **Library** workspace and expand **Templates** and **VM Templates**. Right-click on your VM template and click on **Create Virtual Machine**.

2. Enter a name for the VM. In this case, it is `Tenant A - VM1`. Click on **Next**.

3. On the hardware page, scroll down and click on **Network Adapter**. In the **Connectivity** option, change the selection to **Connected to a VM network**. Click on **Browse**, select **Tenant A** from the dialog, and then click on **OK**.

4. Set the VM subnet to **Subnet 1**.

5. Set the **IP address** section to **Static IP (from a static IP pool)**.

6. Ensure the **MAC address** section is set to **Static**.

7. Under **Port Profile**, change the **Classification** option to **Tenant**.

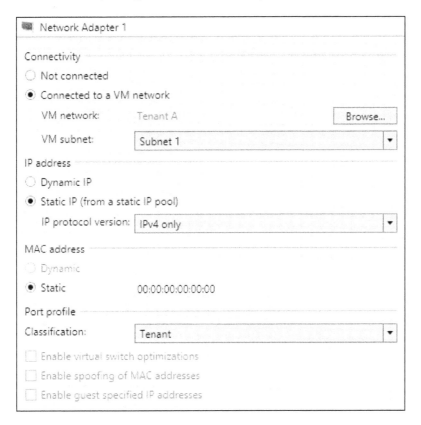

8. Click on **Next**.

9. Change the **Identity Information** field to **TENAVM1** (while this is not necessary, it will make the demonstrations easier). Click on **Next**.

10. Select the destination for the VM; in this case, the **All Hosts\Hosts** group was selected. Click on **Next**.

11. Select which server to deploy the VM to. Click on **Next**.

12. On the **Configure settings** page, select the Network Adapter that was assigned to **VM Network Tenant A**. You will see that you are now able to refine some of the settings from earlier. You can enter the exact IP address from the VM subnet you require, and you can also choose which IP address from the Provider Address Logical Network that is assigned to VM Host. You are also able to choose the MAC address. For this recipe, leave the options blank as VMM will automatically choose the next available IP(s) and MAC addresses. Click on **Next**.

13. On the **Add Properties** page, leave the default options and click on **Next**.

14. Review the summary and click on **Create**.

15. Repeat steps 1-14. However, change the options to reflect **Tenant B**. In step 12, set the **IP address** of the VM network subnet to **10.0.0.3**, as shown in the following screenshot:

16. Once both VMs have been deployed, navigate to the **Fabric** workspace and click on **Logical Networks**. In the ribbon bar, select **Virtual Machines** in the **Show** section. You will be presented with a view similar to the following screenshot:

17. You should see that each VM is now on a different VM network.

18. Right-click on **Tenant A – VM1**, click on **Connect or View**, and then click on **Connect via Console**.

19. Log in to the VM using the local administrator username and password.

20. Open a command prompt in the VM.

21. Type `ipconfig` and press *Enter*. You will see the IP address of the VM, which should be **10.0.0.2**, as shown in the following screenshot:

```
Administrator: Command Prompt                                    — □

Microsoft Windows [Version 6.3.9600]
(c) 2013 Microsoft Corporation. All rights reserved.

C:\Users\Administrator>ipconfig

Windows IP Configuration


Ethernet adapter Ethernet 2:

   Connection-specific DNS Suffix  . :
   Link-local IPv6 Address . . . . . : fe80::354d:c52d:c0cb:19a9%13
   IPv4 Address. . . . . . . . . . . : 10.0.0.2
   Subnet Mask . . . . . . . . . . . : 255.255.255.0
   Default Gateway . . . . . . . . . : 10.0.0.1
```

22. Type `ping 10.0.0.3` and press *Enter*. You will not get a response from the other VM.

```
C:\Users\Administrator>ping 10.0.0.3

Pinging 10.0.0.3 with 32 bytes of data:
Reply from 10.0.0.2: Destination host unreachable.
Reply from 10.0.0.2: Destination host unreachable.
Reply from 10.0.0.2: Destination host unreachable.
Reply from 10.0.0.2: Destination host unreachable.

Ping statistics for 10.0.0.3:
    Packets: Sent = 4, Received = 4, Lost = 0 (0% loss),

C:\Users\Administrator>_
```

Now, you will deploy another VM into Tenant B's VM Network and assign it the 10.0.0.2 IP address.

23. Navigate to **Library | Templates | VM Templates**. Right-click on your VM template and click on **Create Virtual Machine**.

24. Enter a name for the VM. In this case, it is `Tenant B - VM2`. Click on **Next**.

25. On the hardware page, scroll down and click on the Network Adapter. In the **Connectivity** option, change it to **Connected to a VM network**. Click on **Browse**, select **Tenant B** from the dialog, and click on **OK**.

26. Set the VM subnet to **Subnet 1**.

27. Set the **IP address** section to **Static IP (from a static IP pool)**.

28. Ensure **MAC address** is set to **Static**.

29. Under **Port Profile**, change the **Classification** to **Tenant**.

30. Click on **Next**.

31. Change the **Identity Information** field to **TENBVM2** (while this is not necessary it will make the demonstrations easier). Click **Next**.

32. Select the destination for the VM; in this case, the **All Hosts\Hosts** group was selected. Click on **Next**.

33. Select which server to deploy the VM to. Click on **Next**.

34. On the **Configure settings** page, select the Network Adapter that was assigned to the VM Network Tenant B. You will see that you are now able to refine some of the settings from earlier. In the **IPv4 address from VM subnet** field, enter 10.0.0.2. Click on **Next**.

35. On the **Add Properties** page, leave the options as default and click on **Next**.

36. Review the summary and click on **Create**.

37. Now that Tenant B – VM2 has been created, ensure it is started.

38. Right-click on **Tenant B – VM2**, click on **Connect or View**, and then click on **Connect via Console**.

39. Log in to the VM using the local administrator username and password.

40. Open a command prompt in the VM.

41. Type `ipconfig` and press *Enter*. You will see the IP address of the VM, which should be **10.0.0.2**, as shown in the following screenshot:

```
                        Administrator: Command Prompt              —  □

Microsoft Windows [Version 6.3.9600]
(c) 2013 Microsoft Corporation. All rights reserved.

C:\Users\Administrator>ipconfig

Windows IP Configuration


Ethernet adapter Ethernet 2:

   Connection-specific DNS Suffix  . :
   Link-local IPv6 Address . . . . . : fe80::e856:5968:421e:25cc%13
   IPv4 Address. . . . . . . . . . . : 10.0.0.2
   Subnet Mask . . . . . . . . . . . : 255.255.255.0
   Default Gateway . . . . . . . . . : 10.0.0.1
```

42. Type `ping 10.0.0.3` and press *Enter*. You will get a response similar to what is shown in the following screenshot:

```
C:\Users\Administrator>ping 10.0.0.3

Pinging 10.0.0.3 with 32 bytes of data:
Reply from 10.0.0.3: bytes=32 time=2ms TTL=128
Reply from 10.0.0.3: bytes=32 time=1ms TTL=128
Reply from 10.0.0.3: bytes=32 time=1ms TTL=128
Reply from 10.0.0.3: bytes=32 time=1ms TTL=128

Ping statistics for 10.0.0.3:
    Packets: Sent = 4, Received = 4, Lost = 0 (0% loss),
Approximate round trip times in milli-seconds:
    Minimum = 1ms, Maximum = 2ms, Average = 1ms
```

If you do not receive a response, then check the Windows firewall rules on the public profile. Ensure that the rule **File and Printer Sharing (Echo Request - ICMPv4-In)** is enabled.

43. In the same command prompt window, type `arp -a` and press *Enter*. You will see a list of IP addresses and corresponding MAC addresses, as shown in the following screenshot (please note the MAC addresses are likely to be different on your implementation):

```
C:\Users\Administrator>arp -a

Interface: 10.0.0.2 --- 0xd
  Internet Address      Physical Address      Type
  10.0.0.1              00-50-50-d3-d3-8a     dynamic
  10.0.0.3              00-1d-d8-b7-1c-06     dynamic
  10.0.0.255            ff-ff-ff-ff-ff-ff     static
  224.0.0.22            01-00-5e-00-00-16     static
  224.0.0.252           01-00-5e-00-00-fc     static
  255.255.255.255       ff-ff-ff-ff-ff-ff     static
```

44. In the VMM console, click on the **Home** tab in the ribbon bar and then click on the **PowerShell** button. This will launch PowerShell with the VMM module already loaded and the console connected to the current VMM instance. Enter the following PowerShell:

```
$TenantVMs = Get-SCVirtualMachine | Sort-Object
    $($_.VirtualNetworkAdapters.VMNetwork) -Descending

ForEach($VM in $TenantVMs){
    $VM.VirtualNetworkAdapters | Select-Object
        Name,VMNetwork,IPv4Addresses,MACAddress
}
```

45. This will show you a list of the VMs that are currently deployed, the VM Network they are attached to, the IP address(es) assigned, and the MAC address.

Name	VMNetwork	IPv4Addresses	MACAddress
Tenant A - VM1	Tenant A	{10.0.0.2}	00:1D:D8:B7:1C:04
Tenant B - VM2	Tenant B	{10.0.0.2}	00:1D:D8:B7:1C:0B
Tenant B - VM1	Tenant B	{10.0.0.3}	00:1D:D8:B7:1C:06

46. As you can see in the output of the PowerShell, you can see that **Tenant A –VM1** and **Tenant B – VM2** have the same IP address but different MAC addresses.

How it works...

Each VM Network is assigned its own Virtual Subnet ID by VMM, which is then passed down to the Hyper-V servers. As the VM Networks were instructed to use Hyper-V Network Virtualization within the Logical Network "Provider Address", they were instructed to allow VM Networks to use network virtualization. Every time a packet is sent from a VM on either the Tenant A or Tenant B VM Network, it is encapsulated within an NVGRE packet. The following diagram shows how the packet is encapsulated. It has been taken from `http://msdn.microsoft.com/en-us/library/windows/hardware/dn144775(v=vs.85).aspx`.

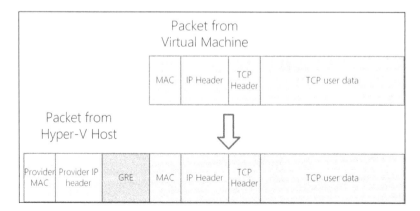

3
Creating the Gateway for Virtual Machine Communications

In this chapter, we will cover the following recipes:

- ▶ Creating a Logical Network, Port Profiles, and Logical Switches for external access
- ▶ Creating a Hyper-V Network Virtualization gateway manually
- ▶ Creating a Hyper-V Network Virtualization gateway with a Service Template

Introduction

HNV requires the use of gateways that understand the **Network Virtualization using Generic Routing Encapsulation** (**NVGRE**) protocol and what is being asked of it.

Microsoft has implemented the gateway functionality within Windows Server 2012 R2, and it is extremely efficient to connect VM Networks to HNV gateways by using VMM.

If you have followed all of the recipes so far in this book, you have a network that logically looks similar to the following diagram:

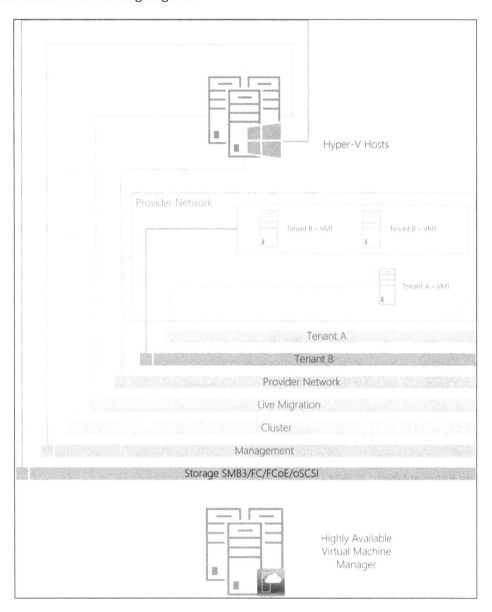

Adding a HNV gateway to this will allow the VMs within the currently declared VM Networks to communicate outside their VM Network. Within Windows Server 2012 R2, there are two possible implementations of the gateway:

- ▸ **Network Address Translation (NAT)**: This is the traditional edge device implementation that allows VMs on the VM Networks to have Internet access and for inbound NAT translation rules. A NAT-based gateway can handle up to 50 VM Networks by default.

- ▸ **Direct Routing**: This acts in a traditional router sense connecting networks together; no form of NAT is performed when this implementation is used and the Tenant IP address is used for all communication. For Direct Routing, a dedicated gateway is required per VM Network.

For the purpose of this chapter, NAT-based gateways are going to be deployed.

Creating a Logical Network, Port Profiles, and Logical Switches for external access

All the Logical Networks that have been defined so far are internal networks and the VMs have no external access. This recipe will show you how to create a Logical Network such that HNV gateways can have external access. The logical structure of the gateway is shown in the following diagram:

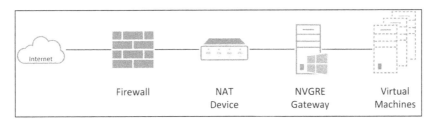

Using HNV gateways behind NAT devices can lead to difficulties in connecting to VPNs. It is advised in a production environment to ensure that gateways are not behind NAT devices.

Getting ready

As the gateway will be behind a NAT device, you will need to ensure that the NAT device is not issuing DHCP-based IP addresses. You will need to know the IP range of the NAT device. In the following recipes, the IP ranges will be as follows:

- ▸ **Subnet**: 192.168.200.0/24
- ▸ **Gateway**: 192.168.200.2

How to do it...

The following diagram shows the high-level steps involved in this recipe:

Overview of Recipe:

Prerequisites (not covered by this recipe):
- Gather all of the VLAN IDs and IP subnets for use in each site for use by External network

Actions:
- Creation of the required Logical Network for External Access
- Creation of a new Uplink Port Profile for the new External Network
- Creation of a new Logical Switch for use by Hyper-V Network Virtualization Gateway hosts

Creating a Logical Network

1. Open the VMM console and navigate to **Fabric | Networking | Logical Networks**. You should have four Logical Networks listed.

Name	Network Compliance	Subnet	Begin Address	End Address
⊟ ᵛᴬᵛ Host-Cluster	Fully compliant			
Host-Cluster-IP-Pool	Fully compliant	172.29.2.0/24	172.29.2.4	172.29.2.254
⊟ ᵛᴬᵛ Host-LiveMigration	Fully compliant			
Host-LiveMigration-IP-Pool	Fully compliant	172.29.1.0/24	172.29.1.4	172.29.1.254
⊟ ᵛᴬᵛ Host-Management	Fully compliant			
Host-Management-IP-Pool	Fully compliant	172.28.0.0/16	172.28.0.101	172.28.0.250
⊟ ᵛᴬᵛ Provider Address	Fully compliant			
PA IPP	Fully compliant	172.30.0.0/16	172.30.0.4	172.30.255.254

2. On the ribbon bar, click on **Create Logical Network**. In the **Name** field, enter `External (NAT)` and enter an appropriate description as well. Ensure the options **One connected network** and **Create a VM network with the same name to allow virtual machines to access the logical network directly** are selected. Click on **Next**.

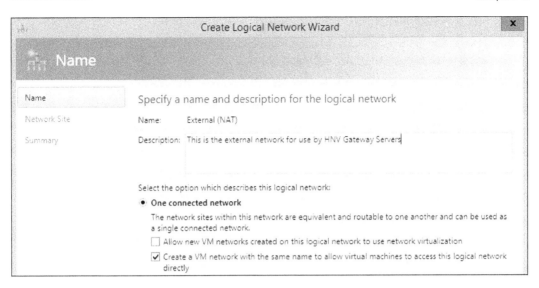

3. On the **Network Site** page, ensure that only the **Gateway** host group is selected. Enter the appropriate VLAN ID and the subnet in use; in this case, **0** and **192.168.200.0/24**. Click on **Next**.

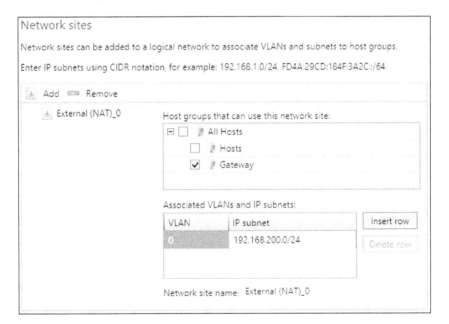

4. Review the summary and click on **Finish**.

5. In the Logical Networks workspace, right-click on the newly created **External (NAT)** Logical Network and click on **Create IP Pool**.

6. Enter an appropriate name, in this case `External (NAT)-IP-Pool`, and a description. Click on **Next**.

7. Ensure that the correct **Network Site** has been selected. Click on **Next**.

8. In the IP address range, enter the range that is available for VMM. In this case, the start IP is `192.168.200.10` and the end IP is `192.168.200.99`. Click on **Next**.

9. Enter the IP address of the gateway for this subnet; in this case, it is `192.168.200.2`. Click on **Next**.

10. Enter the DNS servers. Click on **Next**.

11. Do not enter a WINS server address. Click on **Next**.

12. Review the summary and click on **Finish**.

Creating Uplink Port Profiles

Now that the Logical Network is in place, an Uplink Port Profile is required for the External (NAT) network to function. To achieve this, perform the following steps:

1. In the VMM console, navigate to **Fabric | Networking | Port Profiles**. Right-click on **Port Profiles** and then click on **Create Hyper-V Port Profile**.

2. Enter an appropriate name, in this case `External`, and ensure the **Type of Hyper-V port profile** option is set to **Uplink port profile**. Click on **Next**.

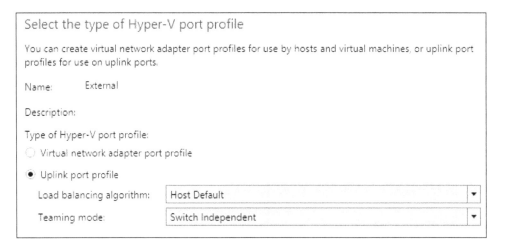

3. Select just the **External (NAT)_0** network site. Click on **Next**.

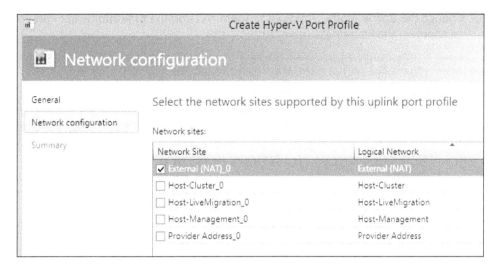

4. Review the summary and click on **Finish**.

5. You should now have two Uplink Port Profiles: **Standard** and **External**.

6. Right-click on **Port Profiles** and click on **Create Hyper-V Port Profile**.

7. Enter an appropriate name, in this case `Provider Network Only`, and ensure the **Type of Hyper-V port profile** option is set to **Uplink port profile**. Click on **Next**.

8. Select just the **Provider Address_0** network site. Click on **Next**.

9. Review the summary and click on **Finish**.

10. You should now have three Uplink Port Profiles: **Standard**, **External**, and **Provider Network Only**.

For the purposes of this recipe, we will use the existing High Bandwidth Adapter Virtual Port Profile; in general, an additional Virtual Port Profile is not required.

Creating Logical Switches

To create Logical Switches, perform the following steps:

1. In the VMM console, navigate to **Fabric** | **Networking** | **Logical Switches**. You will have a single switch listed, **Default**. Right-click on **Logical Switches** and click on **Create Logical Switch**.

2. Review the **Getting Started** page and click on **Next**.

3. Enter an appropriate name, in this case `External`, and a description. Click on **Next**.

4. Do not add any additional extensions and click on **Next**.

5. Change the **Uplink mode** dropdown to **Team** and add the **External** Uplink Port Profile, as shown in the following screenshot:

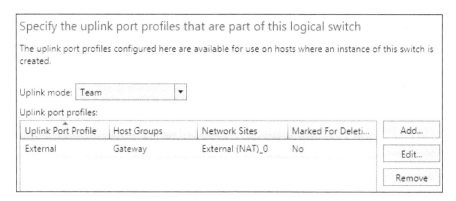

6. Add the **High bandwidth** port classification, and remember to include the **High Bandwidth Adapter** virtual port profile. Click on **OK**.

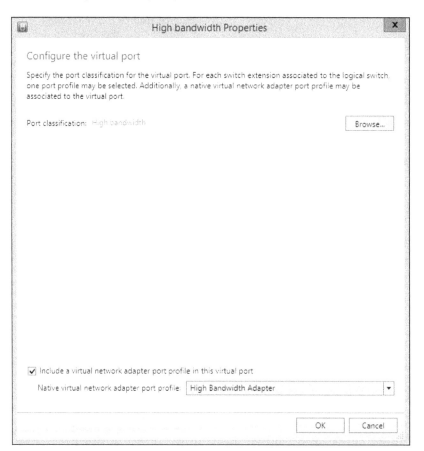

7. Review the summary and click on **Finish.**

8. Right-click on **Logical Switches** and click on **Create Logical Switch**.

9. Review the **Getting Started** page and click on **Next**.

10. Enter an appropriate name, in this case `Tenant Network`, and a description. Click on **Next**.

11. Do not add any additional extensions and click on **Next**.

12. Change the **Uplink mode** dropdown to **Team** and add the **Provider Network Only** Uplink Port Profile.

13. Add the **Tenant** port classification, and remember to include the **Tenant** virtual port profile. Click on **Next**.

14. Review the summary and click on **Finish**.

Now, the following prerequisites are within VMM for the Hyper-V host and the HNV Gateway:

▶ **Logical Network for External communications**: This dictates which Hyper-V server host groups can utilize the underlying Logical Network Sites

▶ **Uplink Port Profiles**: This declares how the Logical Switch is constructed and what physical networks it can use

▶ **Logical Switch**: This defines the Uplink Port Profiles that can be used in the switch and what Virtual Port Profiles are available

How it works...

The creation of the External (NAT) Logical Network will allow Hyper-V Network Virtualization Gateways to connect VMs to networks beyond the previously created Tenant A and Tenant B VM Networks.

Scoping the External (NAT)_0 Logical Network Site exclusively to the Gateway host group ensures that it will not be available to VMs on the core Hyper-V cluster.

Creating a Hyper-V Network Virtualization gateway manually

The HNV gateway is part of the Remote Access role in Windows Server 2012 R2. There is no specific subfeature within the Remote Access role that you can select. This recipe will show you how to create a Virtual Machine that is appropriate for using as a standalone HNV gateway.

Getting ready

You will need to have created a Hyper-V host and added it to VMM within the Gateway host group. This Hyper-V host does not have to be domain joined; if you do not domain join the host, then ensure an appropriate Run As account has been added to VMM for it to manage the host. The existing VMM Run As account would not be suitable as it is a domain account.

This Hyper-V host needs to have at least three NICs. The following diagram shows the logical structure:

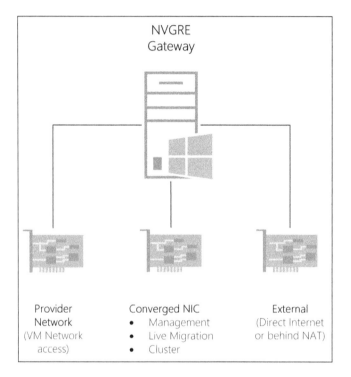

 To learn how to add a Hyper-V host to VMM, please visit `http://technet.microsoft.com/en-us/library/gg610646.aspx`.

Also, you can visit `http://technet.microsoft.com/library/dn423897.aspx` for Microsoft's hardware recommendations for the Windows Server Gateway host.

How to do it...

The following diagram shows the high-level steps involved in this recipe:

Overview of Recipe:

Prerequisites (not covered by this recipe):
- Installation of a Hyper-V host for dedicated Gateway use (min. 3 physical NICs required)
- Adding of the Hyper-V host to VMM

Actions:
- Configuration of the new Hyper-V host to be suitable for hosting Hyper-V Network Virtualization Gateway VMs
- Creation and configuration a new VM to be Hyper-V Network Virtualization Gateway
- Adding the VM to VMM as a Hyper-V Network Virtualization Gateway
- Configuration of the existing VM Networks to use the new VM as a Hyper-V Network Virtualization Gateway

Perform the following steps to create an HNV gateway manually:

1. Navigate to **Fabric | Servers | All Hosts | Gateways**. Right-click on the Hyper-V host that will be the host for the HNV gateway; in this case, it will be **HNVG2**. Click on **Properties**.

2. Click on **Virtual Switches**.

3. Navigate to **New Virtual Switch | New Logical Switch**.

4. Select the **Default** switch from the list of Logical Switches (it should contain **Default** and **External**). Add all the required physical adapters to the Logical Switch, ensuring that the correct adapters are selected.

5. With the Default Logical Switch selected, click on **New Virtual Network Adapter**.

6. Enter an appropriate name; in this case, `Management`. Ensure the option **This virtual network adapter inherits settings from the physical management adapter** is checked. Select the **Host-Management** VM Network and a classification of **Host management**, as shown in the following screenshot:

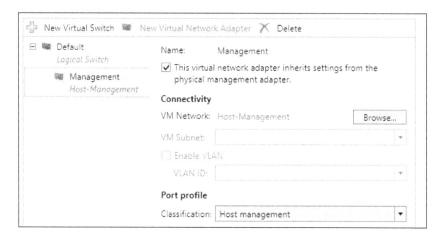

7. Navigate to **New Virtual Switch | New Logical Switch**.

8. Select the **External** switch from the list of Logical Switches (it should contain **Default**, **External**, and **Tenant Network**). Add all the required physical adapters to the Logical Switch, ensuring that the correct adapters are selected. No Virtual Network Adapters will be created on this switch.

9. Navigate to **New Virtual Switch | New Logical Switch**.

10. Select the **Tenant Network** switch from the list of Logical Switches (it should contain **Default**, **External**, and **Tenant Network**). Add all required physical adapters to the Logical Switch, ensuring that the correct adapters are selected. No Virtual Network Adapters will be created on this switch.

11. Click on **OK**.

12. Click on **OK** when the warning about temporary loss of network communication is shown.

13. Once the job is complete, navigate to **Fabric | Servers | All Hosts | Gateway**. Right-click on the Hyper-V host that will be the host for the HNV gateway. Click on **Properties**.

14. Click on **Host Access**.

15. Check the box **This host is a dedicated network virtualization gateway, as a result it is not available for placement of virtual machines requiring network virtualization.** This ensures that VMM will not place, or allow the placement of, any VMs that require HNV on this Hyper-V host; it does not support mixing VMs which require HNV and gateways on the same host. You can place other VMs that do not require HNV on this host, for example VMs that just use VLANs.

16. Click on **OK**.

17. Navigate to **Library | VM templates**, right-click the VM template you created before for use in earlier recipes, and click on **Create Virtual Machine**.

18. Enter an appropriate name, in this case HNVGateway1, and a description. Click on **Next**.

19. Set the current Network Adapter to be connected to the **External (NAT)** VM Network, have a **Static IP** address, have a **Static MAC** address, and use the **High bandwidth** port classification, as shown in the following screenshot:

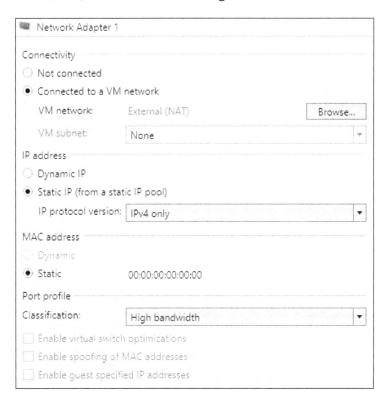

20. Add another Network Adapter to the VM. Set the new Network Adapter to be connected to the Host-Management VM Network, have a **Static IP** address, have a **Static MAC** address, and use the **Host management** port classification.

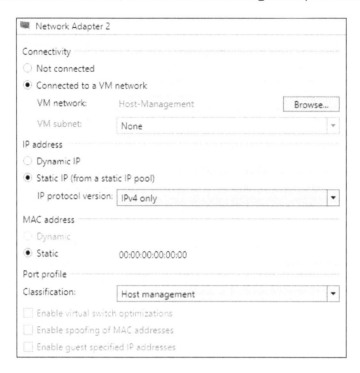

21. Add another Network Adapter to the VM. Set the new Network Adapter status to **Not connected**.

22. Ensure the VM is *not* configured for high availability.

23. Click on **Next**.

24. On the **Configure Operating System** page, enter an appropriate name; in this case, HNVGateway1. Click on **Next**.

25. Select the **Gateway** host group. Click on **Next**.

26. Select the Hyper-V host that was configured with the correct Logical Switches. Click on **Next**.

27. You will be presented with the option to select networks. **Network Adapter 1** and **Network Adapter 2** are configured correctly; however, 3 is not as shown in the following screenshot:

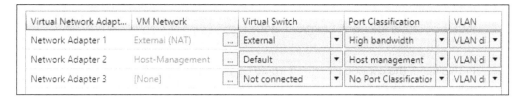

28. Leave the VM Network set to **[None]**, but change the Virtual Switch dropdown to **Tenant Network** and set the VLAN field to **VLAN disabled**:

29. Leave the **Add Properties** page as default and click on **Next**.

30. Review the summary and click on **Create**.

31. Once the VM has been deployed, navigate to **VMs and Services** | **All Hosts** and click the host that has the **HNVGateway1** VM deployed.

32. Right-click on the **HNVGateway1** VM, navigate to **Connect or View**, and click on **Connect via Console**.

33. Log in to the VM if necessary. Open an elevated PowerShell console and enter the following command to install the required Remote Access roles:

```
Install-WindowsFeature -Name DirectAccess-VPN,Routing,RSAT-
RemoteAccess-PowerShell
```

34. In the VMM console, navigate to **Fabric** | **Networking** | **Network Service**. Right-click on **Network Service** and click on **Add Network Service**.

35. Enter an appropriate name, in this case HNVGateway1, and a description. Click on **Next**.

36. Ensure the dropdown **Manufacturer** is set to **Microsoft** and **Model** is set to **Microsoft Windows Server Gateway**. Click on **Next**.

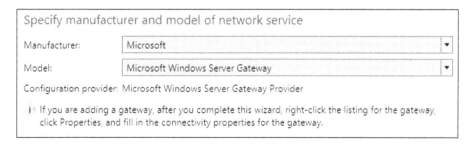

37. Select a Run As account that has sufficient privileges on the HNVGateway1 VM; in this case, the standard **VMM Agent** Run As account. Click on **Next**.

38. In the connection string, enter the information in the requested format:

    ```
    VMHost=<FQDN OF THE HYPER-V HOST>;GatewayVM=<FQDN OF VM TO
       BE THE GATEWAY>
    ```

    In this case, the connection string would be the following:

    ```
    VMHost=HNVG2.ad.demo.com;GatewayVM=hnvgateway1.ad.demo.com
    ```

39. Click on **Next**.

40. Ignore the certificate information as it is not required. Click on **Next**.

41. Click on **Test** to ensure that VMM can utilize the VM. If the VM fails, check the Run As account that was specified has local administrator privileges on the VM. Click on **Next**.

42. Select the **All Hosts** host group as shown in the following screenshot. Click on **Next**.

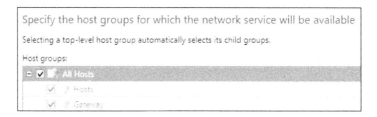

43. Review the summary and click on **Finish**.

44. After the gateway has been added, right-click on the newly created **HNVGateway1** entry and click on **Properties**. Click on the new **Connectivity** option on the left:

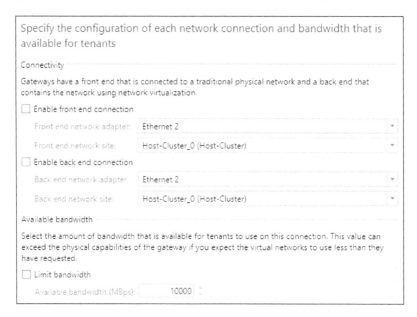

45. It is important to know which network adapter is connected to which network interface. In the wizard, there are the following three Ethernet adapters listed at the moment:

   ❑ **Ethernet2**

   ❑ **Ethernet3**

   ❑ **Ethernet4**

None of these are particularly useful. The following PowerShell script will obtain all the information about the gateway VM from VMM, determine the VM Networks each NIC is attached to and rename the NIC in the VM with the appropriate name. The code is as follows:

```
#Hashtable of VM Networks and the names the NICs should be
    inside the Gateway VM

$NicNames =@{
    "Host-Management" ="Management";
    "External (NAT)"  ="External";
    ""                ="TenantNetworks"
}

#Get the VM from VMM, not from Hyper-V
$GatewayVM = Get-SCVirtualMachine -Name HNVGateway1

#Iterate through each entry in the Hashtable
ForEach($Key in $NicNames.Keys){

    #Find the Network Adapter's MAC Address in VMM that is
        connected to
    #the VM Network. As the Tenant Network Adapter is not
        attached to a
    #VM Network it must be dealt with carefully

    $VNAMacAddress = ($GatewayVM.VirtualNetworkAdapters |
      Where-Object{
        #Check for an actual value
        if($_.VMNetwork.Name){
            if($_.VMNetwork.Name -eq $key){
                $True
            }
        }
```

```
#check for the Tenant NIC
elseif(!($_.VMNetwork.Name) -and !($key)){
    $True
}

}).MACAddress


Invoke-Command -ComputerName $GatewayVM.ComputerName -
    ScriptBlock {
    Param($LocalMacAddress, $NewNicName)
    #Change the format of the MAC Address
    $LocalMacAddress = $LocalMacAddress -replace ":","-
        "
    #Find the NIC based on the MAC address obtained
        from VMM
    $NIC = Get-NetAdapter | Where-Object {
        $_.MacAddress -eq $LocalMacAddress}
    #Get the WMI object based on the NIC's current name
    $wmi = Get-WmiObject -Class Win32_NetworkAdapter -
        Filter "NetConnectionID = ""$($NIC.Name)"""
    #Change the NIC's name to the correct name
    $wmi.NetConnectionID = $NewNicName
    $wmi.Put()
} -ArgumentList $VNAMacAddress,$NicNames.Item($Key)


}
```

46. In the VMM console, click on the **Home** tab in the ribbon bar and click on the **PowerShell** button. This will launch PowerShell with the VMM module already loaded and the console connected to the current VMM instance. In the PowerShell console, execute the script file saved in the previous step.

47. Once the PowerShell script is complete, navigate to **VMs and Services | All Hosts** and click on the host that has the **HNVGateway1** VM deployed.

48. Right-click on the **HNVGateway1** VM, navigate to **Connect or View**, and click on **Connect via Console**.

49. Log in if necessary. Open a command prompt and run `ipconfig`. You will see the names of the Ethernet adapters have changed, as shown in the following screenshot:

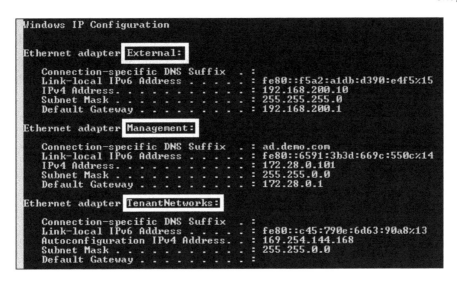

50. Return to the VMM console, navigate to **Fabric | Networking | Network Service**, and right-click on the **HNVGateway1** entry. Click on **Refresh**.

51. Right-click on the **HNVGateway1** entry again and click on **Properties**. Click on the new **Connectivity** option on the left. You will see that the names of the Ethernet adapters have changed, as shown in the following screenshot:

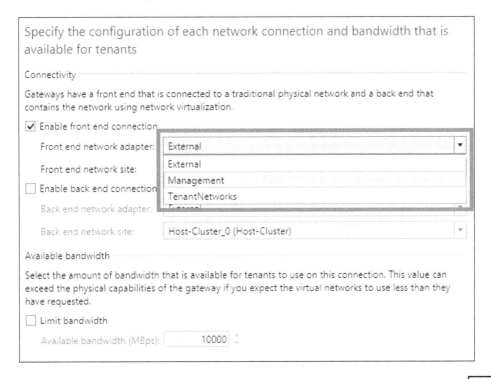

52. Check the **Enable front end connection** checkbox, and then set **Front end network adapter** to **External** and **Front end network site** to **External (NAT)_0 (External (NAT))**.

53. Check the **Enable back end connection** checkbox, and set the **Back end network adapter** to **TenantNetworks** and **Back end network site** to **Provider Address_0 (Provider Address)**, as shown in the following screenshot:

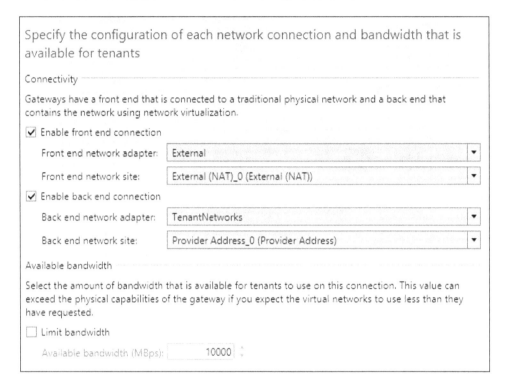

54. Click on **OK**.

55. Now the gateway has been configured, so the existing VM Networks that have been created can be configured to use it for external access. In the VMM console, navigate to **VMs and Service | VM Networks**.

56. Right-click on the **Tenant A** VM Network and click on **Properties**.

57. Click on the **Connectivity** section. You will see that the options have changed.

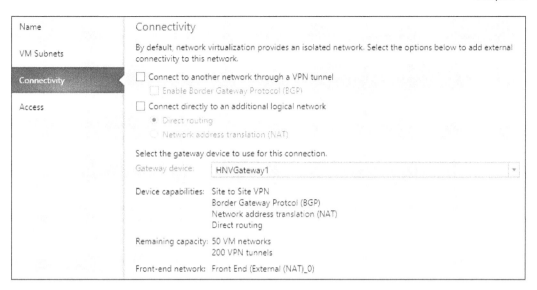

58. Check the **Connect directly to an additional logical network** checkbox and select **Network address translation (NAT)**.

59. You will see a new **Network Address...** section on the left of the dialog. This section allows you to set inbound NAT rules.

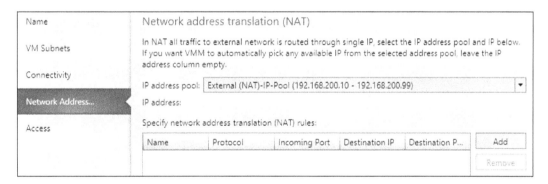

60. Click on **OK**.

61. Navigate to **VMs and Services | All Hosts**.

62. Right-click the **Tenant A – VM 1** VM, navigate to **Connect or View**, and click on **Connect via Console**.

63. Log in if necessary. Open a command prompt and run `ping 4.2.2.2`, as shown in the following screenshot:

```
C:\Users\Administrator>ping 4.2.2.2

Pinging 4.2.2.2 with 32 bytes of data:
Reply from 4.2.2.2: bytes=32 time=19ms TTL=126
Reply from 4.2.2.2: bytes=32 time=11ms TTL=126
Reply from 4.2.2.2: bytes=32 time=17ms TTL=126
Reply from 4.2.2.2: bytes=32 time=13ms TTL=126

Ping statistics for 4.2.2.2:
    Packets: Sent = 4, Received = 4, Lost = 0 (0% loss),
Approximate round trip times in milli-seconds:
    Minimum = 11ms, Maximum = 19ms, Average = 15ms

C:\Users\Administrator>_
```

64. If you try to ping a DNS name such as `www.bing.com`, it will fail as currently there are no DNS servers set in the VM. Run the following PowerShell code inside the **Tenant A – VM 1** VM:

```
Get-NetAdapter | Set-DnsClientServerAddress
-ServerAddresses 4.2.2.2
```

65. You will then be able to ping DNS names such as `www.bing.com` and browse the Internet using DNS names.

```
C:\Windows\system32>ping www.bing.com

Pinging any.edge.bing.com [204.79.197.200] with 32 bytes of data:
Reply from 204.79.197.200: bytes=32 time=11ms TTL=126
Reply from 204.79.197.200: bytes=32 time=9ms TTL=126
Reply from 204.79.197.200: bytes=32 time=16ms TTL=126
Reply from 204.79.197.200: bytes=32 time=17ms TTL=126

Ping statistics for 204.79.197.200:
    Packets: Sent = 4, Received = 4, Lost = 0 (0% loss),
Approximate round trip times in milli-seconds:
    Minimum = 9ms, Maximum = 17ms, Average = 13ms

C:\Windows\system32>_
```

How it works...

The gateway server understands the NVGRE protocol and is able to act as NAT router. By not constraining the TenantNetworks virtual network adapter to a specific VM Network, it is possible for the server to cope with 50 VM Networks (by default)—each with multiple subnets if required. The NVGRE protocol contains the provider's address information, including the Virtual Subnet ID, and the packet within contains the tenant information. This is how the gateway is able to keep data isolated and ensure that even with overlapping subnets, the data is returned to the requesting virtual machine.

The manual process allows you to get familiar with the requirements of an HNV gateway. However, the process can be time consuming and it can be refined using a Service Template.

Creating a Hyper-V Network Virtualization gateway with a Service Template

As we saw in the previous recipe, there is not too much involved in the actual deployment of an HNV gateway. The only required roles/features within the Virtual Machine are:

- ▶ DirectAccess and VPN
- ▶ Routing

It is possible to leverage the Service Template feature within VMM to rapidly provision HNV gateways. However, these gateways will not be available immediately after deployment. This is because they still need to be added to VMM as a Network Service and to the required VM Network(s) as NAT, or Direct Routing and gateways.

Getting ready

You need to have a VM template to use as a basis for the Service Template. The VM template that has been used in previous recipes should be sufficient, provided it is Windows Server 2012 R2 Standard or Datacenter edition with a GUI. (Server Core editions of Windows Server 2012 R2 are not currently supported for use as an HNV gateway.)

How to do it...

The following diagram shows the high-level steps involved in this recipe:

Overview of Recipe:

Actions:
- Creation of single tiered Service Template for deploying a VM capable of being a Hyper-V Network Virtualization Gateway
- Information on where to obtain a prebuilt Service Template to create a highly available Network Virtualization Gateway service

Now, you need to perform the following steps:

1. Open the VMM console.

2. Navigate to **Library | Templates | Service Templates**.

3. Right-click on **Service Templates** and click on **Create Service Template**.

4. Enter an appropriate name for the Service Template, in this case HNV Gateway (non-HA), and a version number, in this case it is 1.0.

5. Under **Patterns**, click on **Single Machine**.

6. Click on **OK**.

7. In the **Service Template Designer** window, drag the VM template to Service Template, as shown in the following screenshot:

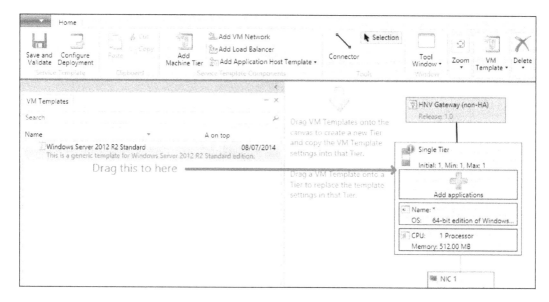

8. Double-click on the tier where you created and click on the **Hardware Configuration** section and add two additional Network Adapters, as shown in the following screenshot:

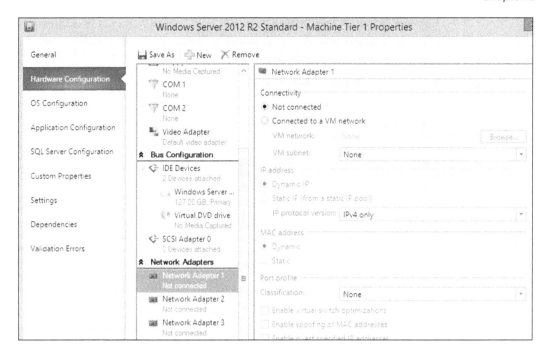

9. Connect **Network Adapter 1** to the **Host-Management** VM Network and set **IP address** to **Static IP**, **MAC address** to **Static**, and **Classification** to **Host management**.

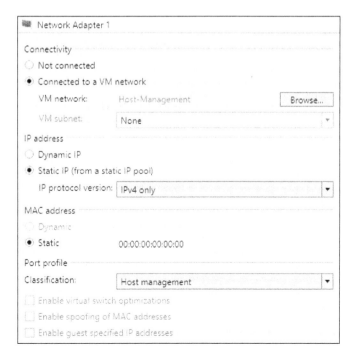

10. Connect **Network Adapter 2** to the **External (NAT)** VM Network and set **IP address** to **Static IP**, **MAC address** to **Static**, and **Classification** to **High bandwidth**.

11. Set **Network Adapter 3** to **Not connected**.

12. Ensure you have four Virtual CPUs and at least 2 GB RAM.

13. Click on the **OS Configuration** section.

14. Set the **Computer** name to HNVGateway## (## will automatically increment the computer name number on each deployment).

15. Under the **Roles** section, check the **Remote Access**, **DirectAccess and VPN (RAS)**, and **Routing** options.

16. Under the **Features** section, check the **Remote Access Management Tools**, **Remote Access GUI and Command-Line Tools**, and **Remote Access module for Windows PowerShell** options.

17. Under the **Networking** option, set the appropriate options to join the VM to the domain.

18. Click on **Save and Validate** to ensure everything is correct.

19. Click on **OK**.

This is sufficient to create a VM with the required Routing and Remote Access Roles and Features for use as an HNV gateway. You will still need to configure VMM as per the previous recipe for it to assign the VM as an HNV gateway.

Using the Microsoft **Web Platform Installer (Web PI)** (http://www.microsoft.com/web/downloads/platform.aspx), it is possible to download a Service Template to create a highly available HNV gateway.

You will need to add the Service Models (http://www.microsoft.com/web/webpi/partners/servicemodels.xml) feed to the Web PI to download the template.

20. Open Web PI.

21. Click on **Options** as shown in the following screenshot:

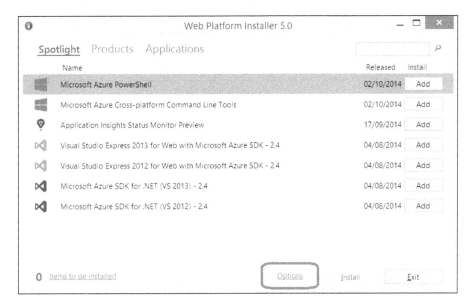

22. In the **Options** dialog, enter the feed to subscribe to in the **Custom Feeds** section, in this case `http://www.microsoft.com/web/webpi/partners/servicemodels.xml`, and then click on **Add feed**.

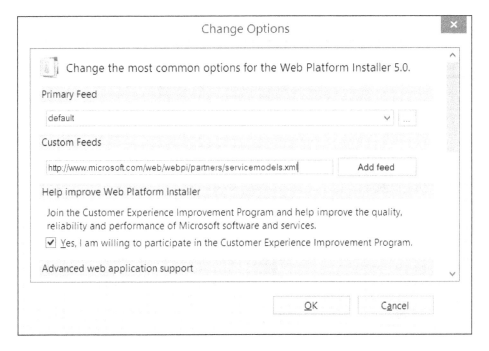

23. Click on **OK**. The Web PI will then refresh itself.

24. Click on **Service Models**.

25. Navigate to **Windows Server 2012 R2 HA Gateway Template**.

26. Click on **Add**.

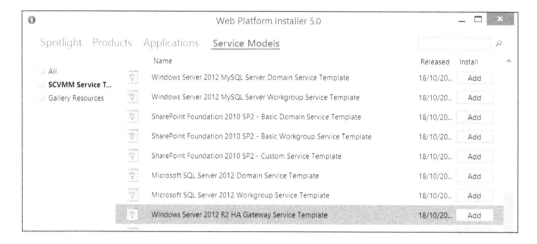

27. Click on **Install**.

28. You will then be presented with the associated license terms. Please review the license and click on **I Accept**.

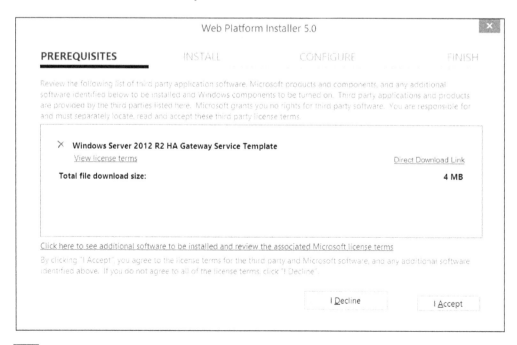

29. Click on **Continue**.

30. Please review the documentation included from Microsoft in the Service Template. This template from Microsoft will show you how to create a highly available HNV gateway.

How it works...

The Service Template functionality within VMM lets VMM take more control of the process. During a Service Template deployment, VMM installs an agent in each VM that forms part of the service. Through this enhanced communication, it is possible for VMM to add additional roles and features to VMs and can therefore save you time.

There's more...

For completely automated deployments of HNV gateways, check out System Center 2012 R2 Orchestrator (`http://technet.microsoft.com/en-us/library/hh237242.aspx`) or Service Management Automation (`http://technet.microsoft.com/en-gb/library/dn469260.aspx`).

4
IP Address Management Integration with VMM for Hyper-V Network Virtualization

In this chapter, we will cover the following recipes:

- ▸ Installing IPAM in Windows Server 2012 R2
- ▸ Integrating IPAM into VMM
- ▸ Using IPAM data for reporting

Introduction

IP Address Management (**IPAM**) was introduced as a feature of Windows Server in Windows Server 2012. Microsoft defines IPAM as follows (`http://technet.microsoft.com/en-gb/library/hh831353.aspx`):

> "...an integrated suite of tools to enable end-to-end planning, deploying, managing and monitoring of your IP address infrastructure, with a rich user experience. IPAM automatically discovers IP address infrastructure servers on your network and enables you to manage them from a central interface."

In Windows Server 2012, IPAM could only integrate with the following:

- ▶ Microsoft Windows DHCP Servers
- ▶ Microsoft Windows DNS Servers
- ▶ Microsoft Windows Network Policy Servers
- ▶ Active Directory Domain Controllers

The minimum version of Windows Server that IPAM will communicate with is Windows Server 2008.

With the introduction of Windows Server 2012 R2, IPAM is able to communicate with System Center 2012 R2 Virtual Machine Manager so that IT administrators can get a complete view of their IP address estate.

The integration with VMM covers any and all IP addresses that VMM can issue—for traditional VLAN-based IP networks as well as for Hyper-V Network Virtualization based networks.

By integrating with IPAM you will be able to get a complete solution for managing and monitoring IP addresses in your IT infrastructure.

Installing IPAM in Windows Server 2012 R2

- ▶ This will be a single server installation of IPAM to allow you to understand the potential capabilities of the feature and what you can do with it.

Getting ready

For this recipe, the following setup is required:

- ▶ A Virtual Machine running Windows Server 2012 R2 Standard or higher with a GUI
- ▶ A new instance of SQL Server for the IPAM database (alternatively, you can use the Windows Internal Database)

Visit `http://technet.microsoft.com/en-us/library/dn758115.aspx` for more details.

How to do it...

The following diagram shows you the high-level steps involved in this recipe:

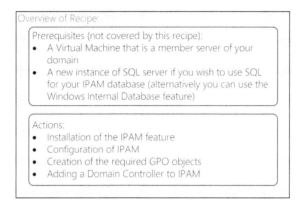

Overview of Recipe:

Prerequisites (not covered by this recipe):
- A Virtual Machine that is a member server of your domain
- A new instance of SQL server if you wish to use SQL for your IPAM database (alternatively you can use the Windows Internal Database feature)

Actions:
- Installation of the IPAM feature
- Configuration of IPAM
- Creation of the required GPO objects
- Adding a Domain Controller to IPAM

1. Launch an elevated PowerShell console on the new server. In this recipe, the server will be **DEMO-IPAM01.**

2. Enter the following PowerShell command:

    ```
    Install-WindowsFeature -Name IPAM -IncludeManagementTools
    ```

3. Open **Server Manager** and click on **IPAM**. You will see the following screen:

4. You will see that you are connected to the local IPAM server and that it is yet to be configured.

5. In the **QUICK START** section, click on **Provision the IPAM Server**.

6. Read the information on the first page of the wizard. Click on **Next**.

7. Enter the appropriate SQL Server information (or if using the Windows Internal Database, select where you would like the database to be stored). Click on **Next**.

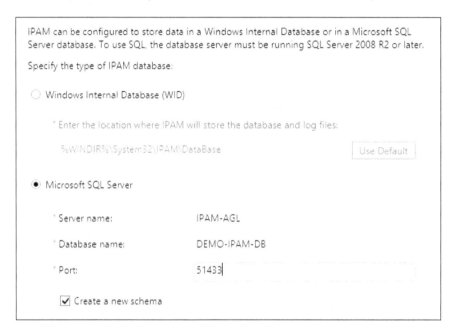

8. Enter the appropriate database credentials for your database. Click on **Next**.

9. For the provisioning method, select **Group Policy Based** and enter an appropriate prefix; in this case, it is DEMO. Click on **Next**.

10. Review the summary information. Click on **Apply**.

11. Click on **Close**.

12. The IPAM console will show several more options, as shown in the following screenshot:

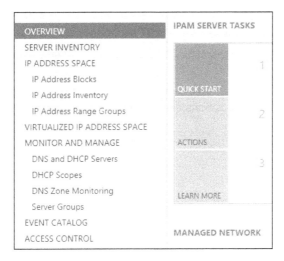

13. The next stage is to configure server discovery. Server discovery defines the domains and functions that the IPAM server will monitor and manage. In the **QUICK START** section, click on **Configure server discovery**.

14. Click on **Add** to select the required domain. Click on **OK**.

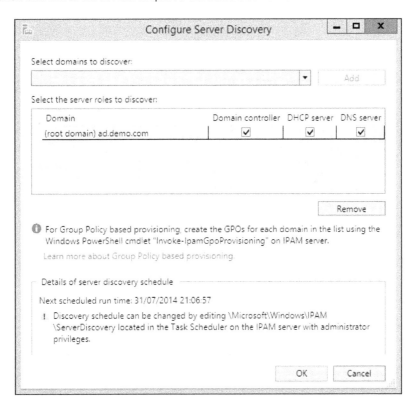

15. In the **QUICK START** section, click on **Start server discovery**. You will see a progress bar across the top of the **QUICK START** section.

16. Once the task is complete, click on **Select or add servers to manage and verify IPAM access**.

17. Right-click on the desired server and click on **Edit Server**. In the next window, ensure the appropriate options are selected. Click on **OK**.

18. You will receive the following error message:

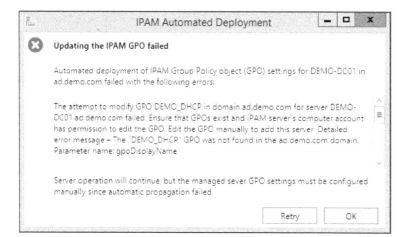

19. Open an elevated PowerShell console, ensure that you have the permissions to create Group Policy Objects, and link them to the root of the domain and run the following PowerShell (all on one line, and substitute the correct domain name, GPO prefix, IPAM server FQDN, and Domain Controller FQDN for yours):

```
Invoke-IpamGpoProvisioning -Domain ad.demo.com -
   GpoPrefixName DEMO -IpamServerFqdn DEMO-
      IPAM01.ad.demo.com -DomainController DEMO-
         DC01.ad.demo.com
```

20. After the GPOs are created, you will need to amend the security filtering on the GPOs to ensure they apply to the correct servers only.

21. Perform a Group Policy Update on the affected servers.

22. You will then need to add the IPAM server to the **Event Log Readers** AD group. This server is located in the **Builtin** container within Active Directory. This is because the IPAM server needs to read logs from Domain Controllers. Execute the following PowerShell on a Domain Controller:

```
Set-ADGroup -Add:@{'Member'=" CN=DEMO-
   IPAM01,OU=Servers,OU=DemoEnv,DC=ad,DC=demo,DC=com"} -
      Identity:"CN=Event Log
         Readers,CN=Builtin,DC=ad,DC=demo,DC=com"
```

23. On the IPAM server, right-click on the server you want and click on **Refresh Server Access Status**.

24. The status should then be **Unblocked**.

25. Right-click on the same server and click on **Retrieve All Server Data**.

This concludes the installation and basic configuration of the IPAM feature.

How it works...

IPAM collects information from all of the Domain Controllers, DNS, and DHCP servers within the specified domain. The Group Policy Objects created by using the `Invoke-IpamGpoProvisioning` cmdlet ensures that the IPAM server has the correct firewall access to the appropriate servers and ensures that the required scheduled tasks are created on the relevant servers.

The information collected by IPAM is stored in its database. IPAM then uses this data to visualize data to the IPAM administrators.

Integrating IPAM into VMM

IPAM is capable of monitoring the IP addresses spaces in VMM to show trend analysis on IP address usage within VMM Logical Network. It is also capable of monitoring physical networks to give you a holistic approach to IP address management. It can show you all the IP addresses that are currently in use across your network in both the physical and virtual environments.

Getting ready

For this recipe, you will require the IPAM server to be installed (this was discussed in the previous recipe). Additionally, you will need a Run As account created in VMM that has the following permissions on the IPAM server:

> **IPAM ASM Administrators**: This is a local group that exists on all IPAM servers and provides permissions for IP **address space management** (**ASM**)

> **Remote Management Users**: This is a built-in group that provides access to WMI resources through management protocols, such as WS-Management through the Windows Remote Management service

In this case, a new user called **SVC_VMMIpam** was created in the ad.demo.com domain and manually added to the two groups above on the IPAM server. This account was added to VMM as a new Run As account called **VMM-IPAM**.

How to do it...

The following diagram shows you the high-level steps involved in this recipe:

1. In the VMM Console, navigate to **Fabric | Networking | Network Service**. Right-click on **Network Service** and click on **Add Network Service**.

2. Enter a name for this connection; in this case, it is DEMO-IPAM01. Click on **Next**.

3. On the **Manufacturer and Model** page, select **Microsoft** as **Manufacturer** and **Microsoft Windows Server IP Address Management** as **Model**, as shown in the following screenshot. Click on **Next**.

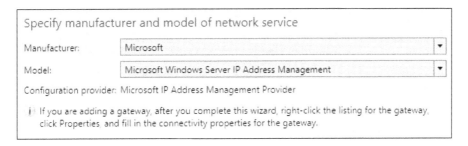

4. Select the Run As account you created earlier; in this case, **VMM-IPAM**. Click on **Next**.

5. Enter the FQDN of the IPAM server; in this case, DEMO-IPAM01.ad.demo.com. Click on **Next**.

6. Ensure the **Configuration provider** field is set to **Microsoft IP Address Management Provider** and click on **Test**. If the test comes back successful, click on **Next**. If any of the tests fails, please ensure the Run As account in VMM has been added to the two groups detailed in the *Getting ready* section for this recipe.

7. Select the Host Groups you want to apply this connection to; in this case, **All Hosts**. Click on **Next**.

8. Review the summary and click on **Finish**.

9. You should now have two Network Services listed in VMM, the first being the **HNVGateway1** service added in the previous chapter and the second being the new IPAM service (**DEMO-IPAM01**), as shown in the following screenshot:

10. On the IPAM server, in this case **DEMO-IPAM01**, open **Server Manager**.

11. Navigate to the **IPAM** section. Click on **VIRTUALIZED IP ADDRESS SPACE**.

The following table can help you interpret some of the information that you see on the IPAM server (`http://technet.microsoft.com/en-gb/library/dn249418.aspx`):

VMM name	IPAM name
Logical network	VIRTUALIZED IP ADDRESS SPACE Provider IP Address Space: VMM Logical Network column
Network site	VIRTUALIZED IP ADDRESS SPACE Provider IP Address Space: Network Site column
IP address subnet	IP Address Subnet (same name in IPAM as in VMM)
IP address pool	IP Address Range
VM network	VIRTUALIZED IP ADDRESS SPACE Customer IP Address Space: VM Network column

How it works...

IPAM and VMM have bidirectional communication through the use of the configured Run As account; in this case, VMM-IPAM. By adding the IPAM server to VMM, it is possible to monitor and even configure logical networks, their network sites, and IP pools. By integrating IPAM with VMM, you will be able to monitor all networks—both physical and software defined—within your organization.

Tenants, such as Tenant A and Tenant B, should not use IPAM to configure their networks and must use VMM.

Using IPAM data for reporting

IPAM has a wealth of information for managing and monitoring your IP address space. Many basic pieces of information can be seen in the IPAM client interface; however, it is also possible to export data from IPAM in CSV format.

Getting ready

It is advisable to create several new VMs in VMM for each Tenant VM Network to establish some trend data.

You will need access to a Windows PC with Microsoft Excel 2013 installed to utilize the information exported in CSV format.

How to do it...

The following diagram shows you the high-level steps involved in this recipe:

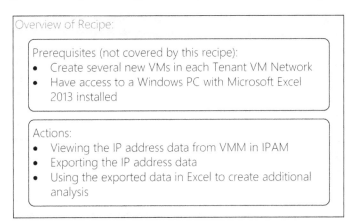

1. Open the IPAM client on the IPAM server and navigate to **VIRTUALIZED IP ADDRESS SPACE**, as shown in the following screenshot:

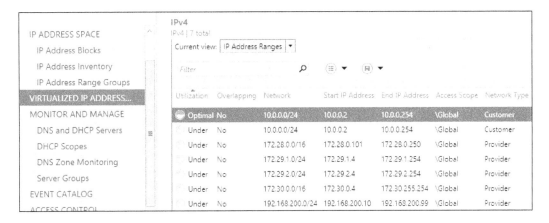

2. Selecting the subnet for the VM Network for Tenant A, you will see a variety of information in the details view beneath:

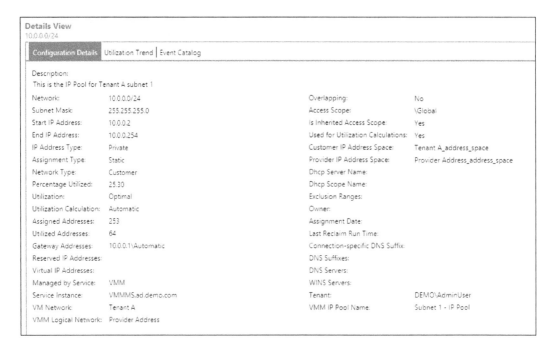

3. It is possible to see the details that were entered in VMM; however, IPAM will show you the utilization status of the subnet in terms of the actual number of IP addresses used and that number expressed as a percentage of the overall number of addresses.

4. Click on the **Utilization Trend** tab.

5. Select a range to view the trend analysis for, as shown in the following screenshot:

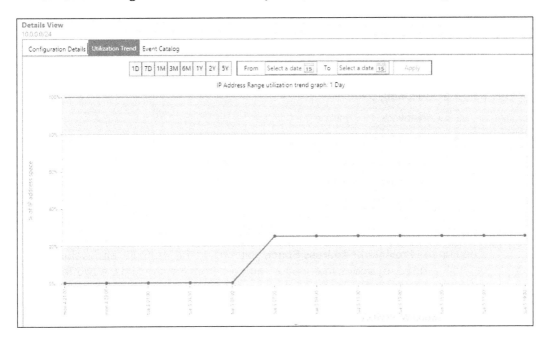

6. This will show you how the usage of IP addresses within the VM Network has been trending.

7. Above the details view, where the subnets are listed, click on **TASKS** on the top right-hand corner and click on **Export**.

8. Select the location to save the CSV and enter a file name. Click on **Save**.

9. Copy the CSV file to the PC where you have Microsoft Excel 2013 installed.

10. Open the CSV file in Excel.

11. You will see that all of the data shown in the details view is on the same line as the subnet.

12. Select the following columns:

  ❏ C: Network

  ❏ K: Provider IP Address Space

  ❏ O: Percentage Utilized

  ❏ P: Assigned Addresses

  ❏ Q: Utilized Addresses

13. Copy these columns to a new worksheet in Excel.

14. Clean up the **Provider IP Address Space** columns. In this example, each value had the _address_space information removed from the end and the two Tenant networks were named correctly, as shown in the following screenshot:

	A	B	C	D	E
1	Provider IP Address Space	Network	Percentage Utilized	Assigned Addresses	Utilized Addresses
2	Tenant A	10.0.0.0/24	25.29644269	253	64
3	Tenant B	10.0.0.0/24	17.78656126	253	45
4	Host-Management	172.28.0.0/16	0.666666667	150	1
5	Host-LiveMigration	172.29.1.0/24	0.796812749	251	2
6	Host-Cluster	172.29.2.0/24	0.796812749	251	2
7	Provider Address	172.30.0.0/16	0.007629977	65531	109
8	External (NAT)	192.168.200.0/24	3.333333333	90	3

15. Click on the **Insert** tab on the ribbon bar.

16. Click on **Recommended Charts**.

17. Excel will show you a variety of charts it can create based on the data presented on the worksheet.

18. For this example, select **100% Stacked Bar**. Click on **OK**.

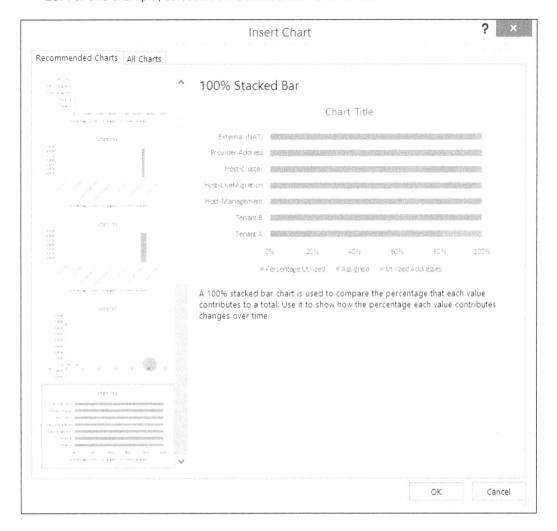

19. This will insert a chart object into your Excel worksheet.

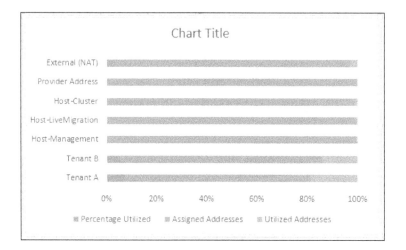

20. This chart can then be altered as required within Excel and utilized in other applications as required. This can include colors, width, height, and so on.

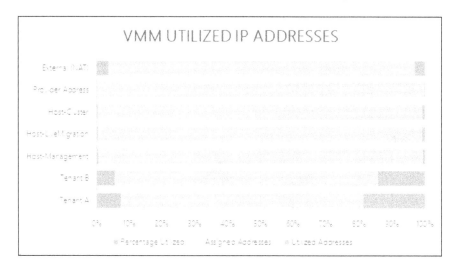

How it works...

As IPAM has all of the available data from VMM, it can be used to monitor IP address usage in VMM defined networks. It is possible to use PowerShell to export the data from IPAM.

Excel is capable of providing rich data visualizations and can give you the ability to slice data as appropriate. This can lead to high-quality management information reporting.

5
Windows Server Gateway Configuration

In this chapter, we will cover the following recipes:

- ▸ Network Address Translation (NAT) with the gateway
- ▸ Direct Routing and how it is different from NAT

Introduction

Windows Server 2012 R2 includes an inbox gateway solution for **Hyper-V Network Virtualization (HNV)** within the Routing and Remote Access server role.

As HNV uses the NVGRE protocol, a gateway server must be able to understand the protocol and undertake the required functions. If a gateway is configured to use **Network Address Translation (NAT)**, it will mask the internal HNV network behind the NAT interface.

If a gateway is configured for Direct Routing, then it will perform the decapsulation of network packets leaving an HNV network and also the encapsulation of data entering an HNV network.

Network Address Translation with the gateway

In *Chapter 3*, *Creating the Gateway for Virtual Machine Communications*, you created a Windows Server Gateway so that VMs could access resources outside of the VM Network they resided upon. This access was only one way: outbound; this recipe will show you how to create inbound NAT rules on the gateway to allow access to your VM's resources. A typical use case of this would be to host a website behind a public IP address.

In this recipe, you will create a simple web server and publish it using NAT rules on the Windows Server Gateway.

Getting ready

For this recipe, you will need access to a computer that is outside of the VM Networks created so far, but it can access the IP range you used for the external network.

How to do it...

The following diagram shows you the high-level steps involved in this recipe:

Overview of Recipe:

Prerequisites (not covered by this recipe):
- Have access to a computer that can access the External (NAT) network

Actions:
- Install IIS on a test VM in the Tenant A VM Network
- Create a custom HTML page
- Create a NAT rule to the test VM
- Test the NAT rule
- View the configuration change in the Windows Server Gateway

Now, perform the following steps:

1. Start a Tenant A VM on your Hyper-V cluster; in this case, **Tenant A – VM 10**.

2. Once the VM has started, log on to the VM using an administrative account.

3. Open an elevated PowerShell window and enter the following PowerShell and press *Enter*:

    ```
    Install-WindowsFeature Web-Server,Web-WebServer,Web-Common-
        Http,Web-Default-Doc,Web-Dir-Browsing,Web-Http-Errors,Web-
            Static-Content,Web-Health,Web-Http-Logging,Web-
                Performance,Web-Stat-Compression,Web-Security,Web-
                    Filtering,Web-Mgmt-Tools,Web-Mgmt-Console
    ```

4. This will then install IIS with the required features for this recipe, as shown in the following screenshot:

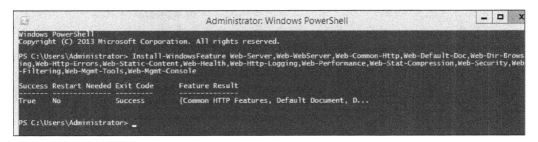

5. Once IIS is complete, open Internet Explorer and go to the URL `http://localhost`. You will be greeted with the default IIS page.

6. Open an elevated Notepad window.

7. Enter the following HTML code between the `<body>` and `</body>` tags. Please enter some text of your choosing. Make a note of the text you have entered. Some example code is as follows:

    ```
    <HTML>
    <HEAD>
      <TITLE>HNV Testing</TITLE>
    <HEAD>
    <BODY>
    <h1>Software Defined Networking Rocks!</h1>
    <p>This is some test text for the Hyper-V Network
      Virtualization Cookbook!</p>
    </BODY>
    </HMTL>
    ```

8. Save this file as `HNV.htm` in `C:\InetPub\wwwroot`, as shown in the following screenshot:

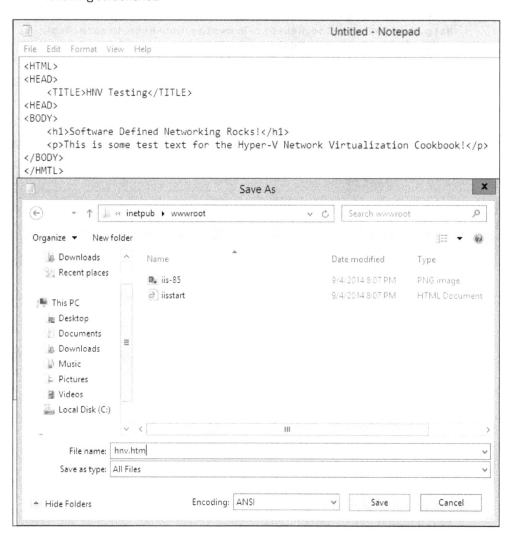

9. Open Internet Explorer and go to the URL `http://localhost/hnv.htm`. You should see the text you entered in step 7.

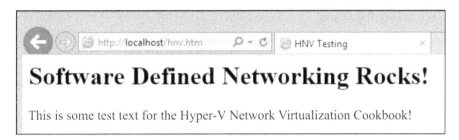

10. On the VMM server, open the VMM console.

11. Open the **VMs and Services** workspace and navigate to **All Hosts** | **Hosts** | **hypvclus01**.

12. Find the VM you have just installed IIS on, as shown in the following screenshot:

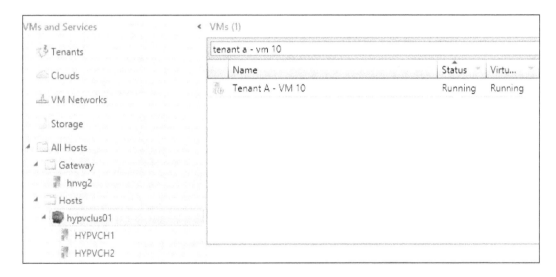

13. Right-click on the VM and click on **Properties**.

14. Click on **Hardware Configuration**, scroll down to **Network Adapters**, click on **Network Adapter 1**, and then click on **Connection Details**. This will show you the IP address the VM has been assigned from the VM network (disregard the IPv6 address). Make a note of this IP address.

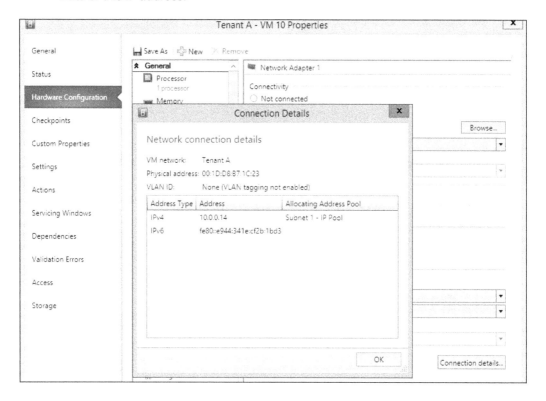

15. Click on **OK** to close the **Connection Details** dialog.

16. Click on **Cancel** to close the VM properties.

17. Within the **VMs and Services** workspace, click on **VM Networks**.

18. Right-click on the **Tenant A** VM Network.

19. Click on **Properties**.

20. Click on the **Network Address Translation (NAT)** option. You will see there are no entries in there, as shown in the following screenshot:

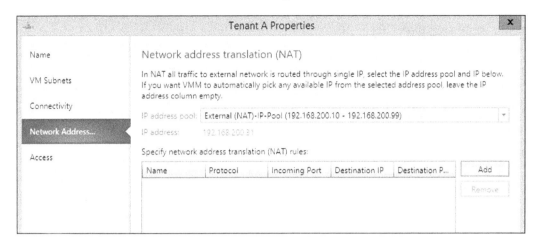

21. Make a note of the IP address that has been issued to this VM Network; in this case, **192.168.200.31**.

22. Click on **Add**.

23. Add a rule with the following parameters:

    ❑ Name: **WWW Test**

    ❑ Protocol: **TCP**

    ❑ Incoming Port: **80**

    ❑ Destination IP: **10.0.0.14** (please use the IP address obtained in step 14)

    ❑ Destination Port: **80**

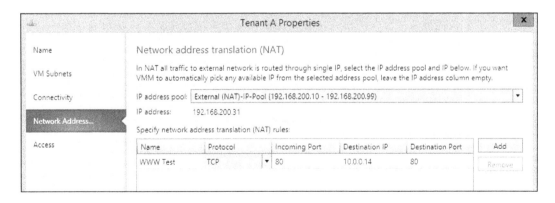

24. Click on **OK**.

25. This has now created a new NAT rule for this VM Network only.

26. On a machine that has access to the External (NAT) address, in this case `192.168.200.31`, open Internet Explorer.

27. Navigate to `http://192.168.200.31/hnv.htm`. You should see the text you entered in step 7.

28. To see what VMM has done to make this work, open a PowerShell console on the VMM server.

29. Type in the following cmdlet:

```
Enter-PSSession HNVGateway1
```

30. Provided the account you are using has permissions to log on to the HNVGateway1 server, you will see the PS Console change to have a prefix of **[HNVGateway1]**.

31. Type in the following cmdlet:

```
Get-NetNatStaticMapping
```

32. You will then see the configuration that VMM has applied to the Windows Server Gateway:

```
                                                        Windows PowerShell
Windows PowerShell
Copyright (C) 2013 Microsoft Corporation. All rights reserved.

PS C:\Users\adminuser> Enter-PSSession HNVGateway1
[HNVGateway1]: PS C:\Users\adminuser\Documents> Get-NetNatStaticMapping

StaticMappingID             : 0
NatName                     : a18eeff9-bd7f-46bd-b313-d825983d2df9
Protocol                    : TCP
RemoteExternalIPAddressPrefix : 0.0.0.0/0
ExternalIPAddress           : 192.168.200.31
ExternalPort                : 80
InternalIPAddress           : 10.0.0.14
InternalPort                : 80
InternalRoutingDomainId     : {00000000-0000-0000-0000-000000000000}
Active                      : True


[HNVGateway1]: PS C:\Users\adminuser\Documents> _
```

As you can see, the **External IP Address** has been set to **192.168.200.31**, the **External Port** has been set to **80**, the **Internal IP Address** has been set to **10.0.0.14**, and the **Internal Port** has been set to **80**.

33. Type in the following cmdlet:

```
Get-NetNatSession
```

34. You will then see the current sessions using this NAT rule:

```
[HNVGateway1]: PS C:\Users\adminuser\Documents> Get-NetNatSession

NatName                     : a18eeff9-bd7f-46bd-b313-d825983d2df9
InternalRoutingDomainId     : {a18eeff9-bd7f-46bd-b313-d825983d2df9}
CreationTime                : 04/09/2014 20:28:48
Protocol                    : 6
InternalSourceAddress       : 10.0.0.14
InternalSourcePort          : 80
InternalDestinationAddress  : 192.168.200.1
InternalDestinationPort     : 52198
ExternalSourceAddress       : 192.168.200.31
ExternalSourcePort          : 80
ExternalDestinationAddress  : 192.168.200.1
ExternalDestinationPort     : 52198
```

The **External IP address** can be seen to be **192.168.200.1**, which is where the website was visited from.

How it works...

Network Address Translation (NAT) within **Hyper-V Network Virtualization (HNV)** is very similar to traditional NAT. When the Windows Server Gateway is connected to VMM, it is provisioned in multitenant mode. In addition to knowing the destination IP address and port number for the inbound traffic, the Windows Server Gateway combined with the Hyper-V host wraps the traffic in the NVGRE protocol. This allows the traffic to be routed on the physical network using the Provider Address network to ensure the traffic arrives on the Hyper-V host where the destination machine is residing.

Direct Routing and how it is different from NAT

Direct Routing does not mask the VM Network to external networks unlike NAT, which can expose port numbers and then direct that traffic to the correct VM and (optionally) a different port.

Direct Routing works more like a traditional router and as such a Windows Server Gateway that is configured in Direct Routing mode can only support a single VM Network, whereas Windows Server Gateways configured for NAT can support up to 50 VM Networks by default.

In this recipe, you will create a simple web server and it will be available to computers outside of the HNV network using its HNV IP address; NAT will not be used.

Getting ready

You should have completed the *Creating HNV Gateways with Service Templates* recipe in *Chapter 3*, *Creating the Gateway for Virtual Machine Communications*, as this recipe relies upon the service template that was created in that recipe.

A new Windows Server Gateway will be provisioned for use by this recipe as it will be dedicated to the Tenant B VM Network.

How to do it...

The following diagram shows you the high-level steps involved in this recipe:

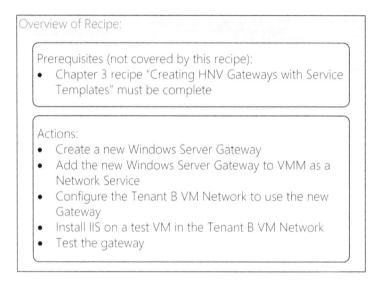

Now, perform the following steps:

1. Open the VMM Console, navigate to the **Library** workspace, and click on **Service Templates**. You should have the **HNV Gateway (non-HA)** Service Template listed, as shown in the following screenshot:

2. Right-click on the **HNV Gateway (non-HA)** Service Template and click on **Configure Deployment**.

3. Enter an appropriate name, `HNVGateway2` in this case, and ensure the destination host group is set to **Gateway**. Click on **OK**.

4. In the **Deploy Service** preview, click on the HNVGateway instance, change **VM name** to `HNVGateway2.ad.demo.com`, and change **Computer name** to `HNVGateway2.ad.demo.com`, as shown in the following screenshot:

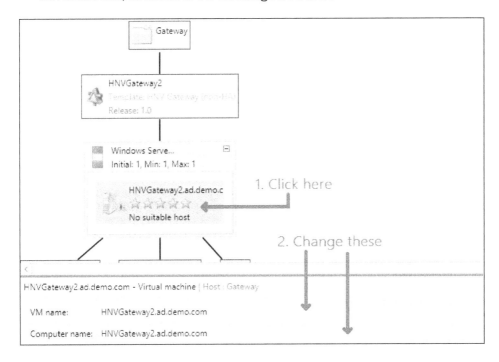

5. Beneath **Computer name**, click on the select button and choose the **HNVG2** host. Click **OK**.

6. On the ribbon bar, click on **Refresh Preview**.

7. Prior to deploying the service, it is suggested to prestage the Computer account in Active Directory, ensuring it is in the correct OU to receive the relevant Group Policy to set local administrators.

8. On the ribbon bar, click on **Deploy Service**.

9. When asked if you're sure you want to deploy the service, click on **Deploy**.

10. After the Service has been deployed, navigate to **VMs and Services**.

11. Find the **HNVGateway2.ad.demo.com** VM. Right-click on the VM and click on **Properties**.

12. Click on **Hardware Configuration** and scroll down to **Network Adapters**. On the Network Adapter that is not connected, click on **Connected to a VM network**.

13. Click on the **Browse** button.

14. Click on **Clear selection**.

15. Click on **OK**.

16. You will then be able to set **Standard Switch** as **TenantNetwork**.

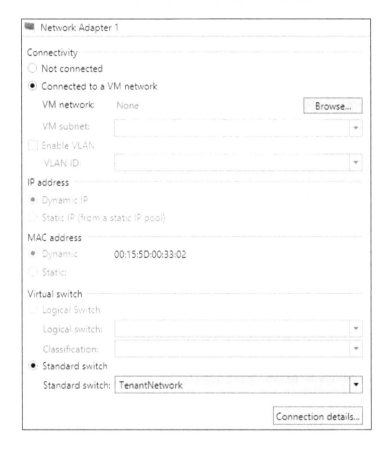

17. Click on the network adapter that is connected to the **External (NAT)** VM Network.

18. Click on **Connection details**.

19. Make a note of the IP address (disregard the IPv6 address); in this case, the IP address is **192.168.200.32**:

20. Click on **OK** to close the **Connection Details** dialog.

21. To close the VM properties, click on **OK**.

22. Navigate to the **Fabric** workspace.

23. Expand **Networking**, then right-click on **Network Service**.

24. Click on **Add Network Service**.

25. Enter an appropriate name; in this case, `HNVGateway2`. Click on **Next**.

26. Select **Microsoft** as **Manufacturer**.

27. Set **Microsoft Windows Server Gateway** as **Model**.

28. Click on **Next**.

29. In the **Credentials** section, select the correct VMM Run As account; in this case, **VMM Agent Run As**. Click on **Next**.

30. In the **Connection String** option, you need to enter additional information for Direct Routing to work correctly:

```
VMHost=HNVG2.ad.demo.com;GatewayVM=HNVGateway2.ad.demo.com;
   BackendSwitch=TenantNetwork;DirectRoutingMode=True;
      FrontEndServerAddress=192.168.200.32
```

Ensure the IP address is the same as obtained in step 19.

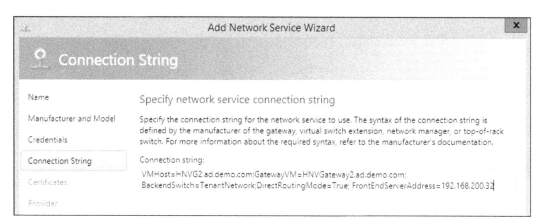

31. Click on **Next**.

32. Click on **Next**.

33. On the provider screen, click on **Test**. Ensure tests are passed.

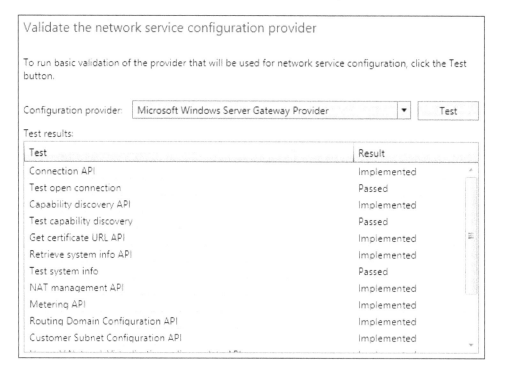

34. Click on **Next**.

35. Select **All Hosts**. Click on **Next**.

36. Review the summary and click on **Finish**.

37. Using the PowerShell script from *Chapter 3*, *Creating the Gateway for Virtual Machine Communications*, change the name of the VM to `HNVGateway2.ad.demo.com`:

```
#Hashtable of VM Networks and the names the NICs should be
  inside the Gateway VM

$NicNames =@{
    "Host-Management" ="Management";
    "External (NAT)"  ="External";
    ""                ="TenantNetworks"
}

#Get the VM from VMM, not from Hyper-V
$GatewayVM = Get-SCVirtualMachine -Name
  HNVGateway2.ad.demo.com

#Iterate through each entry in the Hashtable
ForEach($Key in $NicNames.Keys){

    #Find the Network Adapter's MAC Address in VMM that is
      connected to
    #the VM Network. As the Tenant Network Adapter is not
      attached to a
    #VM Network it must be dealt with carefully

    $VNAMacAddress = ($GatewayVM.VirtualNetworkAdapters |
      Where-Object{
        #Check for an actual value
        if($_.VMNetwork.Name){
            if($_.VMNetwork.Name -eq $key){
                $True
            }
        }
        #check for the Tenant NIC
        elseif(!($_.VMNetwork.Name) -and !($key)){
            $True
        }

    }).MACAddress


    Invoke-Command -ComputerName $GatewayVM.ComputerName -
      ScriptBlock {
```

```
                    Param($LocalMacAddress, $NewNicName)
                    #Change the format of the MAC Address
                    $LocalMacAddress = $LocalMacAddress -replace ":","-
                      "
                    #Find the NIC based on the MAC address obtained
                      from VMM
                    $NIC = Get-NetAdapter | Where-Object {
                      $_.MacAddress -eq $LocalMacAddress}
                    #Get the WMI object based on the NIC's current name
                    $wmi = Get-WmiObject -Class Win32_NetworkAdapter -
                      Filter "NetConnectionID = ""$($NIC.Name)"""
                    #Change the NIC's name to the correct name
                    $wmi.NetConnectionID = $NewNicName
                    $wmi.Put()
               } -ArgumentList $VNAMacAddress,$NicNames.Item($Key)



          }
```

38. In the VMM console, click on the **Home** tab in the ribbon bar and click on the PowerShell button. This will launch PowerShell with the VMM module already loaded and the console connected to the current VMM instance. In the PowerShell console execute the script.

39. In the PowerShell console, run the following cmdlet:

```
Get-SCNetworkService -Name "HNVGateway2" | Read-SCNetworkService
```

40. Once the script is complete, run the following PowerShell script to configure HNVGateway2:

```
#Get the VMM Run As account
$credentials = Get-SCRunAsAccount -Name "VMM Agent Run As"
#Get the Windows Server Gateway Provider
$configurationProvider = Get-SCConfigurationProvider -Name
  "Microsoft Windows Server Gateway Provider"
#Get the current HNVGateway2 configuration
$networkService = Get-SCNetworkService -Name "HNVGateway2"
#Get the External network adapter
$frontEndAdapter = $networkService.NetworkAdapters |
  ?{$_.AdapterName -eq "External"}
#Get the External (NAT) logical network
```

```
$logicalNetwork = Get-SCLogicalNetwork -Name "External
  (NAT)"
#Get the appropriate site
$frontEnd = Get-SCLogicalNetworkDefinition -Name "External
  (NAT)_0" -LogicalNetwork $logicalNetwork
#Define the Front End Connection
Add-SCNetworkConnection -Name "Front End" -
  LogicalNetworkDefinition $frontEnd -Service
    $networkService -NetworkAdapter $frontEndAdapter -
      ConnectionType "FrontEnd" -RunAsynchronously


#Get the TenantNetworks network adapter
$backEndAdapter = $networkService.NetworkAdapters |
  ?{$_.AdapterName -eq "TenantNetworks"}
#Get the Provider Address network
$logicalNetwork = Get-SCLogicalNetwork -Name "Provider
  Address"
#Get the appropriate site
$backEnd = Get-SCLogicalNetworkDefinition -Name "Provider
  Address_0" -LogicalNetwork $logicalNetwork
#Define the Back End Connection
Add-SCNetworkConnection -Name "Back End" -
  LogicalNetworkDefinition $backEnd -Service
    $networkService -NetworkAdapter $backEndAdapter -
      ConnectionType "BackEnd" -RunAsynchronously
#Update the Network Service
Set-SCNetworkService -NetworkService $networkService -Name
  "HNVGateway2" -Description "" -ConnectionString
    "VMHost=HNVG2.ad.demo.com;GatewayVM=HNVGateway2.ad.demo.com
      ; BackendSwitch=TenantNetwork;DirectRoutingMode=True;
        FrontEndServerAddress=192.168.200.32" -RunAsAccount
          $credentials
```

41. HNVGateway2 is now ready to use as a direct router.

42. In the VMM console, navigate to the **VMs and Service** workspace, click on **VM Networks**, and right-click on the **Tenant B** VM Network. Click on **Properties**.

43. Click on **Connectivity** and check the **Connect directly to an additional logical network** checkbox. Select the **Direct routing** option and select **HNVGateway2** as **Gateway device**. Click on **OK**.

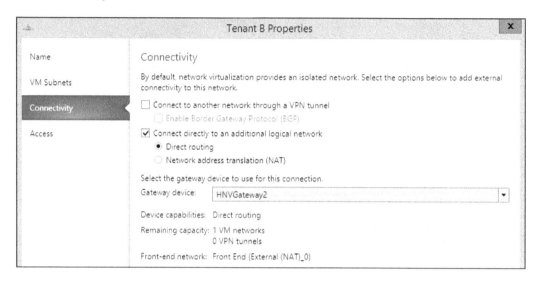

44. In the VMM Console, open the **VMs and Services** workspace, navigate to **All Hosts | Hosts | hypvclus01**.

45. Select a Tenant B VM at random; in this case, **Tenant B – VM 10**.

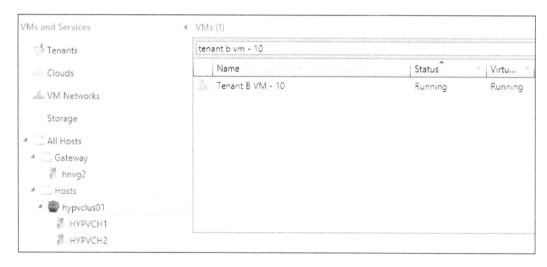

46. Right-click on the VM, navigate to **Connect or View | Connect via Console**.

47. Log in to the VM using an administrative account.

48. Open an elevated PowerShell window, enter the following PowerShell, and press *Enter*:

```
Install-WindowsFeature Web-Server,Web-WebServer,Web-Common-
Http,Web-Default-Doc,Web-Dir-Browsing,Web-Http-Errors,Web-Static-
Content,Web-Health,Web-Http-Logging,Web-Performance,Web-Stat-
Compression,Web-Security,Web-Filtering,Web-Mgmt-Tools,Web-Mgmt-
Console
```

49. This will then install IIS with the required features for this recipe.

50. Once IIS is complete, open Internet Explorer and go to the URL `http://localhost`. You will be greeted with the default IIS page.

51. Open an elevated Notepad window.

52. Enter the following HTML code between the `<body>` and `</body>` tags. Please enter some text of your choosing. Make a note of the text you have entered:

```
<HTML>
<HEAD>
   <TITLE>HNV Testing for Direct Routing</TITLE>
<HEAD>
<BODY>
<h1>Software Defined Networking Rocks!</h1>
<h2>Direct Routing is easy!</h2>
<p>This is some more test text for the Hyper-V Network
Virtualization Cookbook!</p>
</BODY>
</HMTL>
```

53. Save this file as `HNV.htm` in `C:\InetPub\wwwroot`.

54. Open Internet Explorer and go to the URL `http://localhost/hnv.htm`. You should see the text you entered in step 52:

55. Open a command prompt in the VM and enter `ipconfig`. Make a note of the IP address. In this case, the IP address is **10.0.0.3**.

56. Return to the machine you used in step 26 in the *Network Address Translation with the Gateway* recipe. This machine should have access to the **External (NAT)** network; in this case, the 192.168.200.0/24 network.

57. Open Internet Explorer and navigate to `http://10.0.0.3/hnv.htm`.

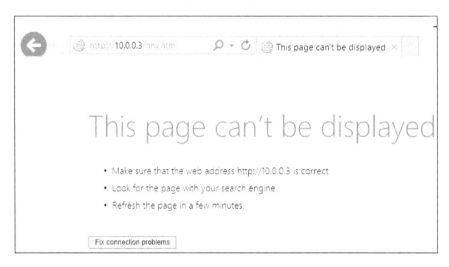

58. This will fail as this machine does not know how to access the `10.0.0.0/24` network. Leave Internet Explorer open.

59. On this machine, open an elevated PowerShell console.

60. Enter the following PowerShell cmdlet:

```
Get-NetRoute -DestinationPrefix 192.168.200.0/24
```

61. If you receive an error, then you will need to speak to your Network Administrator to determine how your machine routes to that network. Consider you receive the following reply:

```
PS C:\WINDOWS\system32> Get-NetRoute -DestinationPrefix 192.168.200.0/24

ifIndex DestinationPrefix                                    NextHop
------- -----------------                                    -------
31      192.168.200.0/24                                     0.0.0.0
```

Then, you will be able to continue with this recipe.

62. Make a note of the **ifIndex** value that has been returned, as this is the Interface Index the machine uses to route traffic outside of its local subnet. Run the following PowerShell cmdlet:

```
New-NetRoute -DestinationPrefix 10.0.0.3/32 -InterfaceIndex
    31 -AddressFamily IPv4 -NextHop 192.168.200.32
```

In this, `10.0.0.3` is the IP address of the VM you have installed IIS on, 192.168.200.32 is the IP address of the External (NAT) interface on `HNVGateway2.ad.demo.com`, and the `InterfaceIndex` value is the **ifIndex** value returned in step 61.

63. Return to Internet Explorer and press *F5* to refresh the page. You will get the following screenshot:

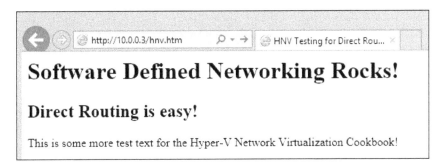

64. In the PowerShell console you have open, enter the following command:

```
Tracert 10.0.0.3
```

65. You should receive the following information. If you do not receive this information, then check that the VM either has its firewall disabled or the **File and Printer Sharing (Echo Request – ICMPv4-In)** rule is enabled:

```
PS C:\WINDOWS\system32> tracert 10.0.0.3

Tracing route to TENBVM10 [10.0.0.3]
over a maximum of 30 hops:

  1    <1 ms    <1 ms    <1 ms   HNVGATEWAY2 [192.168.200.32]
  2     4 ms     5 ms     9 ms   TENBVM10 [10.0.0.3]
  3     3 ms     3 ms     3 ms   TENBVM10 [10.0.0.3]
```

66. You will see that none of the routing information returned contains the Provider IP addresses for HNVGateway2 or the VM.

How it works...

Direct Routing within HNV is very similar to traditional routing. When the Windows Server Gateway is connected to VMM, it is provisioned in routing mode.

The Windows Server Gateway combined with the Hyper-V host wraps the inbound traffic in the NVGRE protocol. This allows the traffic to be routed on the physical network using the Provider Address network to ensure the traffic arrives on the Hyper-V host where the destination machine is residing.

Outbound traffic has the NVGRE header information removed from packets as they leave the gateway server, and the recipients of this traffic are unaware that the source is actually contained within an HNV network.

6
Implementing Network Isolation in Hyper-V

In this chapter we will cover the following recipes:

- ▶ Understanding VLANs in Hyper-V and VMM, including the PowerShell cmdlets
- ▶ Understanding Private VLANs in Hyper-V and VMM, including the PowerShell cmdlets

Introduction

In addition to Hyper-V Network Virtualization (HNV), it is possible to achieve network isolation using traditional VLANs and Private VLANs.

VLAN tags are added by the Hyper-V Extensible Switch and not by the guest operating system inside the VM. VMs are not aware that their traffic is being tagged. Private VLANs offer a different type of isolation, which can help break a VLAN into multiple sub-VLANs.

In the case of Private VLANs, VMs are unaware of their participation in a Private VLAN.

Understanding VLANs in Hyper-V and VMM, including the PowerShell cmdlets

VLANs in Hyper-V allow for the isolation of traffic. It is possible to set a network adapter to trunk VLANs into a VM; an example use case for this could be a network load balancer that is responsible for multiple VLANs.

Getting ready

In this recipe you will be creating additional VLANs in VMM and will require a new VLAN ID and subnet.

How to do it...

The following diagram shows you the high-level steps involved in this recipe:

Overview of Recipe:

Prerequisites (not covered by this recipe):
- Determine which VLAN IDs to create in VMM

Actions:
- Creation of a Logical Network for VLAN Isolation
- Creating of a Logical Network Site with 2 VLANs
- Creating 2 VM Networks for VLANs
- Creating a VM in one of the new VLANs

This table shows you the VLANs and the settings that will be applied:

Setting Name	Value	
Logical Network Name	VLAN Testing	
Logical Network Site Name	VLAN Testing_0	
VLAN ID	150	151
IP subnet	192.168.150.0/24	192.168.151.0/24
IP pool name	IPP-VLAN_Testing_0-150	IPP-VLAN_Testing_0-151
IP pool start address	192.168.150.2	192.168.151.2
IP pool end address	192.168.150.254	192.168.151.254
VM Network Name	VMN-VLAN_Testing_0-150	VMN-VLAN_Testing_0-151

Now perform the following steps:

1. Open the VMM Console and navigate to **Fabric | Networking | Logical Networks**. You should have five Logical Networks listed, as shown in the following diagram:

Name	Network Compliance	Subnet	Begin Address	End Address
Logical Networks and IP Pools (5)				
⊟ ᴧ External (NAT)	Fully compliant			
External (NAT)-IP-Pool	Fully compliant	192.168.200.0/24	192.168.200.10	192.168.200.99
⊟ ᴧ Host-Cluster	Fully compliant			
Host-Cluster-IP-Pool	Fully compliant	172.29.2.0/24	172.29.2.4	172.29.2.254
⊟ ᴧ Host-LiveMigration	Fully compliant			
Host-LiveMigration-IP-Pool	Fully compliant	172.29.1.0/24	172.29.1.4	172.29.1.254
⊟ ᴧ Host-Management	Fully compliant			
Host-Management-IP-Pool	Fully compliant	172.28.0.0/16	172.28.0.101	172.28.0.250
⊟ ᴧ Provider Address	Fully compliant			
PA IPP	Fully compliant	172.30.0.0/16	172.30.0.4	172.30.255.254

2. On the ribbon bar click on **Create Logical Network**.

3. Enter a name and a description for the Logical Network, in this case `VLAN Testing`, and ensure the **VLAN-based independent networks** option is selected. Click on **Next**.

> ● **VLAN-based independent networks**
>
> The subnet-VLAN pairs defined by the sites in this logical network are used as independent networks. They might or might not be routable to one another.

4. Create a Logical Network Site; however, declare two subnets for the site. In this case, **VLAN 150** and **151** are using **192.168.150.0/24** and **192.168.151.0/24**, respectively. Click on **Next**.

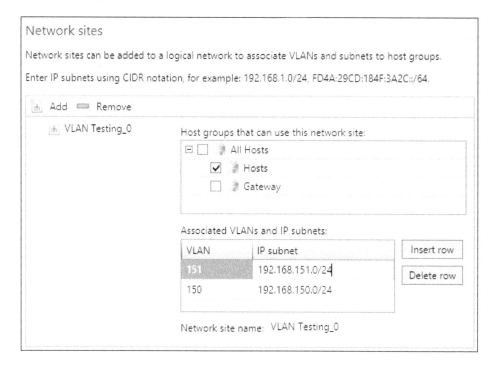

5. Review the summary and click on **Finish**.

6. To create the IP pool for the new Logical Network Site, right-click on **VLAN Testing** and click on **Create IP Pool**.

7. Enter a name and description, in this case, IPP-VLAN_Testing_0-151, and click on **Next**.

8. Select **192.168.151.0/24** from the **IP subnet** drop-down list and click on **Next**.

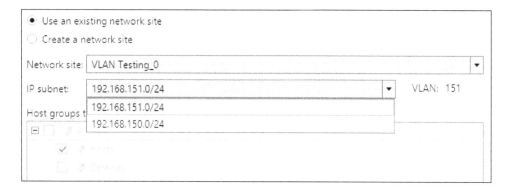

9. Enter a start and end IP address, in this case, `192.168.151.2` and `192.168.151.254`, respectively. Click on **Next**.

10. Complete the remaining pages of the wizard, leaving the settings as default or blank.

11. Create another IP pool, but this time for the **192.168.150.0./24** subnet, following the instructions in the previously mentioned steps, 6-10, using the IP pool name `IPP-VLAN_Testing_0-150`. Once complete, your Logical Network settings should be displayed as a table at the start of this recipe, as shown in the following screenshot:

⊟ VLAN Testing	Fully compliant			
IPP_VLAN_Testing_0-150	Fully compliant	192.168.150.0/24	192.168.150.2	192.168.150.254
IPP-VLAN_Testing_0-151	Fully compliant	192.168.151.0/24	192.168.151.2	192.168.151.254

IPP_VLAN_Testing_0-150

Static IP address pool information		IP address usage	
Starting address:	192.168.150.2	Available addresses:	252
Ending address:	192.168.150.254	Available for dedicated IP addresses:	252
Reserved addresses:	0	Available virtual IP addresses:	0
Virtual IP address range:		Total addresses:	253
		Total dedicated IP addresses:	253
Host groups		Total virtual IP addresses:	0
All Hosts\Gateway			
All Hosts\Hosts			

12. Right-click on the Logical Network **VLAN Testing** and click on **Create VM Network**.

13. Enter an appropriate name, in this case, `VMN-VLAN_Testing_0-150`, and click on **Next**.

Specify a name and description for the VM network

Name: VMN-VLAN_Testing_0-150

Description:

14. On the isolation page select the **Specify a VLAN** option and select the **192.168.150.0/24-150** network (**-150** denotes the VLAN ID). Click on **Next**.

15. Review the summary and click on **Finish**.

16. Repeat steps 12-14 for the other subnet (**192.168.151.0/24-151**) by calling the VM Network `VMN-VLAN_Testing_0-151`.

17. Navigate to the **VMs and Services** workspace and click on **VM Networks**. You should have eight VM Networks listed, as shown in the following screenshot:

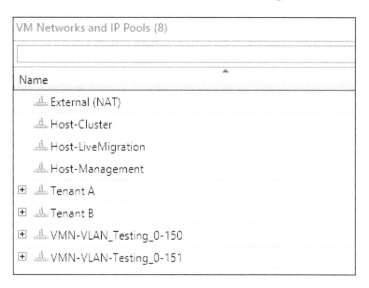

18. Click on the **+** sign next to **Tenant A** and **VMN-VLAN-Testing_0-150** to show the IP subnets beneath the VM Networks.

19. You will see that the **VMN-VLAN-Testing_0-150** IP pool is linked to the IP pool created in steps 6-10 and creates a dependency between the Logical Network, its Logical Network Site, IP pool, and then the VM Network. This reflects non-software defined networking.

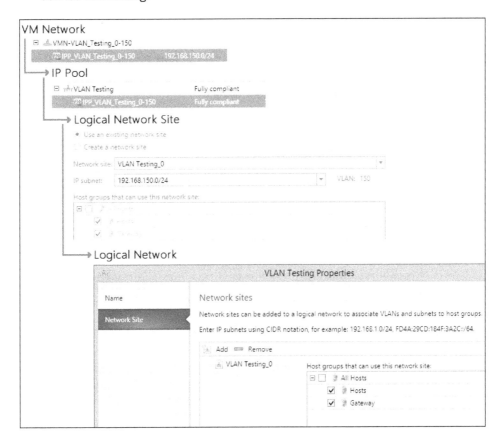

20. You will see that the **Tenant A Subnet 1 – IP Pool** is only linked to the VM Network, which allows subnets to be created within the VM Network without having to change the underlying Logical Network, Logical Network Sites, and provider IP pool. This is software-defined networking.

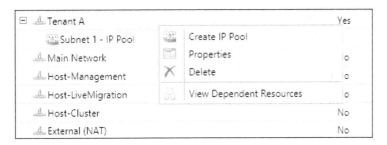

Any Virtual Machines created in the **VMN-VLAN-Testing_0-150** or **VMN-VLAN-Testing_0-151** VM Networks are isolated in that VLAN. Any traffic between those VLANs must traverse the default gateway for those VLANs, which would more than likely be a physical router away from the Hyper-V environment.

To add this VLAN to the Standard Uplink Port Profile, which controls the Logical Switches, perform the following steps:

21. Navigate to the **Fabric** workspace and then click on **Port Profiles**. Right-click on the **Standard** UPLINK PORT PROFILE and click on **Network Configuration**.

22. Click on **VLAN-Testing_0** and then click on **OK**.

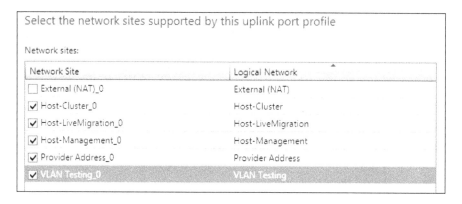

23. This tells VMM that the VLANs are now available wherever this uplink port profile is used.

24. To test whether the VLANs are available navigate to the **Library** workspace; click on **VM Templates**; right-click on your default VM template, in this case, **Windows Server 2012 R2 Standard**; and then click on **Create Virtual Machine**.

25. Navigate through the **Create Virtual Machine** wizard giving the appropriate information. Use a suitable name, in this case, VLAN150-1. Ensure that the VM is connected to **VM Network VMN-VLAN-Testing_0-150** and the **VMN-VLAN-Testing_0-150_0** VM subnet is selected on the **Configure Hardware** page, as shown in the following screenshot:

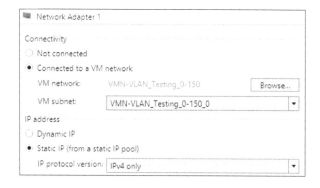

26. Complete the deployment of the Virtual Machine.

27. Once the VM has been deployed, navigate to the **VMs and Services** workspace, and click on **All Hosts.**

28. Start one of your VMs that use Hyper-V Network Virtualization, in this case, **Tenant A – VM 1**, and live migrate it to the same host as **VLAN150- 1VM**. This will show you that two different isolation technologies can be used on the same Hyper-V host.

29. Once the VM has completed its live migration, open a PowerShell console on the VMM server. Note that this does not need to be an elevated PowerShell console.

30. Once you have opened PowerShell, type in `Enter-PSSession HYPVCH1` and press *Enter* (where `HYPVCH1` is the name of the Hyper-V host where both VMs are running). You will see the PowerShell session change, as shown in the following screenshot:

```
                                                          Windows PowerShell

Windows PowerShell
Copyright (C) 2013 Microsoft Corporation. All rights reserved.

PS C:\Users\adminuser> Enter-PSSession HYPVCH1
[HYPVCH1]: PS C:\Users\AdminUser\Documents>
```

31. The prefix **[HYVCH1]** indicates that any further PowerShell you execute in this console will be executed on HYPVCH1 until you exit the remote PowerShell session.

32. Enter the following PowerShell and press *Enter*:

```
Get-VM | Where State -eq "Running"
```

33. This will return a list of running VMs: in this case, the list should include **Tenant A – VM 1** and **VLAN150-1**, as shown in the following screenshot:

```
[HYPVCH1]: PS C:\Users\AdminUser\Documents> Get-VM | Where State -eq "Running"

Name            State    CPUUsage(%) MemoryAssigned(M) Uptime    Status
----            -----    ----------- ----------------- ------    ------
Tenant A - VM 1 Running 0            512                02:03:38 Operating normally
VLAN150-1       Running 0            512                01:46:17 Operating normally
```

34. Enter the following PowerShell and press *Enter*:

```
Get-VM | Where State -eq "Running" | Get-VMNetworkAdapter |
    FL
```

35. This will show you the details of each network adapter in each Virtual Machine.

```
PS C:\Windows\system32> Get-VM | Where State -eq "Running" | Get-VMNetworkAdapter | FL

Name                      : Tenant A - VM 1
Id                        : Microsoft:924D5814-7A99-4E15-A283-4F144D69073F\A2354181-11EA-4574-AED9-7D8FC91F91F3
IsLegacy                  : False
IsManagementOs            : False
ComputerName              : HYPVCH1
VMName                    : Tenant A - VM 1
VMId                      : 924d5814-7a99-4e15-a283-4f144d69073f
SwitchName                : Default
SwitchId                  : 9bb43391-3e85-4ce2-8fbd-c723fc54c6c3
Connected                 : True
PoolName                  :
MacAddress                : 001DD8B71C1A
DynamicMacAddressEnabled  : False
MacAddressSpoofing        : Off
AllowTeaming              : Off
RouterGuard               : Off
DhcpGuard                 : Off
StormLimit                : 0
PortMirroringMode         : None
IeeePriorityTag           : Off
VirtualSubnetId           : 4490741
DynamicIPAddressLimit     : 0
VMQWeight                 : 0
VMQUsage                  : 0
IOVWeight                 : 0
IOVUsage                  : 0
IovQueuePairsRequested    : 1
IovQueuePairsAssigned     : 0
IOVInterruptModeration    : Default
IPsecOffloadMaxSA         : 0
IPsecOffloadSAUsage       : 0
VFDataPathActive          : False
MaximumBandwidth          : 0bps
MinimumBandwidthAbsolute  : 0bps
MinimumBandwidthWeight    : 1(weight)
BandwidthPercentage       : 0%
MandatoryFeatureId        : {}
MandatoryFeatureName      : {}
Status                    : {Ok}
IPAddresses               : {10.0.0.5, fe80::51bb:deec:e14e:6356}

Name                      : VLAN150-1
Id                        : Microsoft:E474D00E-B3E8-45CF-9816-18D4C63AFE7C\CFDFB29A-78A7-4215-9AC8-5FDAFA0D3639
IsLegacy                  : False
IsManagementOs            : False
ComputerName              : HYPVCH1
VMName                    : VLAN150-1
VMId                      : e474d00e-b3e8-45cf-9816-18d4c63afe7c
SwitchName                : Default
SwitchId                  : 9bb43391-3e85-4ce2-8fbd-c723fc54c6c3
Connected                 : True
PoolName                  :
MacAddress                : 001DD8B71C59
DynamicMacAddressEnabled  : False
MacAddressSpoofing        : Off
AllowTeaming              : Off
RouterGuard               : Off
DhcpGuard                 : Off
StormLimit                : 0
PortMirroringMode         : None
IeeePriorityTag           : Off
VirtualSubnetId           : 0
```

How it works...

VLANs in Hyper-V work just as VLANs do in the physical network. The VLAN assigned to the VM network adapter is tagged when network traffic leaves a VM and is removed when traffic enters. In this respect the VLAN acts like a native VLAN on a switch port. It is possible to trunk VLANs into a VM using PowerShell; please see this TechNet article for trunking VLANs http://technet.microsoft.com/en-us/library/hh848475.aspx.

Understanding Private VLANs in Hyper-V and VMM, including the PowerShell cmdlets

Private VLANs (PVLANs) divide a typical VLAN into sub-VLANs while maintaining the IP subnet and Layer 3 configuration. Each sub-VLAN can become its own isolation boundary based on the port type.

Hyper-V has the capability of supporting the following Private VLAN port types:

- **Promiscuous**: This type of port is permitted to communicate to any other port within a PVLAN including Isolated and Community

- **Isolated**: This type of port is only permitted to communicate to Promiscuous ports within a PVLAN and cannot communicate other Isolated ports or Community ports

- **Community**: This type of port is permitted to communicate with any other Promiscuous or Community port within the PVLAN

PVLANs separate traffic at Layer 2. The following diagram describes the port types:

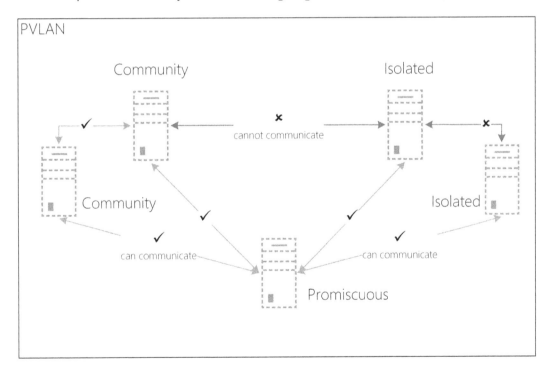

- Unfortunately System Center 2012 R2 Virtual Machine Manager only supports Isolated PVLANs.

Getting ready

In this recipe you will be creating additional VLANs in VMM and will require a new VLAN ID and subnet. Additionally a PVLAN will be created.

How to do it...

The following diagram shows you the high-level steps involved in this recipe:

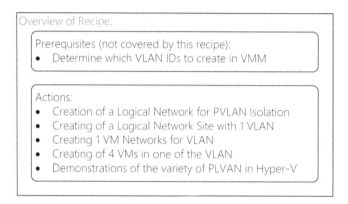

Now perform the following steps:

1. Open the VMM Console and navigate to **Fabric | Networking | Logical Networks**. You should have six Logical Networks listed, as shown in the following screenshot:

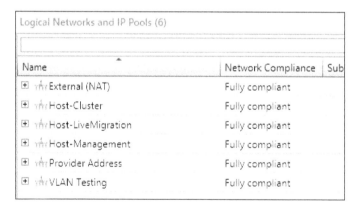

2. On the ribbon bar click on **Create Logical Network**.

3. Enter a name and a description for the Logical Network, in this case, `PVLAN Testing`, and ensure the **Private VLAN (PVLAN) networks** option is selected. Click on **Next**.

⦿ **Private VLAN (PVLAN) networks**

The network sites within this logical network contain independent networks consisting of primary and secondary VLAN pairs in isolated mode.

---

4. When you are presented with the **Network sites** page, click on **Add**. You will see a new column, **Secondary VLAN**, under the **Associated VLANs and IP subnets** section. Enter the appropriate information for your PVLAN, in this case, the VLAN ID is 190, the secondary VLAN is 5, and the subnet is `192.168.190.0/24`. Ensure the **All Hosts** host group is selected. Click on **Next**.

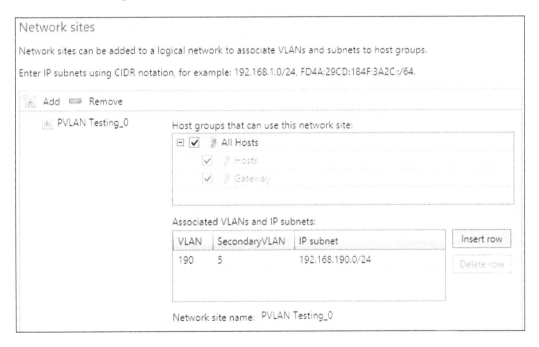

5. Review the summary and click on **Finish**.

6. To create the IP pool for the new Logical Network Site, right-click on **PVLAN Testing** and click on **Create IP Pool**.

7. Enter a name and description, in this case, `IPP-PVLAN_Testing_0-190`, and click on **Next**.

8. On the **IP address range** page, enter a start and end IP address, in this case, `192.168.190.2` and `192.168.190.254` respectively, and then click on **Next**.

9. Complete the remaining pages of the wizard with the default options.

10. Right-click on the Logical Network **PVLAN Testing** and click on **Create VM Network**.

11. Enter an appropriate name, in this case, `VMN-PVLAN_Testing_0-190`, and click on **Next**.

Specify a name and description for the VM network

Name: VMN-PVLAN_Testing_0-190

Description:

---

12. On the isolation page, select the **Specify a VLAN** option and select the **192.168.190.0/24-190 5** network (**-190** denotes the VLAN ID and **5** denotes the Secondary VLAN). Then click on **Next**.

13. Review the summary and click on **Finish**.

14. Navigate to the **Fabric** workspace, and then click on **Port Profiles**. Right-click on the **Standard** uplink port profile and click on **Network Configuration**.

15. Click on **PVLAN-Testing_0**. Then click on **OK**.

Select the network sites supported by this uplink port profile

Network sites:

Network Site	Logical Network
☐ External (NAT)_0	External (NAT)
☑ Host-Cluster_0	Host-Cluster
☑ Host-LiveMigration_0	Host-LiveMigration
☑ Host-Management_0	Host-Management
☑ Provider Address_0	Provider Address
☑ PVLAN Testing_0	PVLAN Testing
☑ VLAN Testing_0	VLAN Testing

---

16. This tells VMM that the newly created PVLANs are now available wherever this uplink port profile is used.

17. Navigate to the **Library** workspace, click on **VM Templates**, and right-click on your default VM template, in this case, **Windows Server 2012 R2 Standard**. Then click on **Create Virtual Machine**.

18. Navigate through the **Create Virtual Machine** wizard giving the appropriate information. Use a suitable name, in this case `PVLAN190-1`. On the **Configure Hardware** page ensure the VM is connected to the VM Network **VMN-PVLAN-Testing_0-190** and that the **VMN-PVLAN-Testing_0-190_0** subnet is selected on **Network Adapter 1**, as shown in the following screenshot:

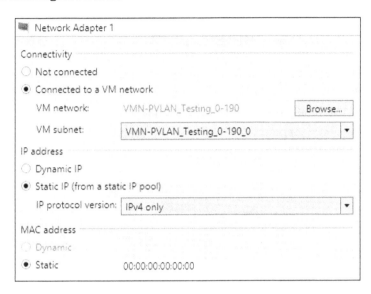

19. Complete the deployment of the Virtual Machine.

20. Repeat steps 17-19 three times for a total of four VMs on the **VMN-PVLAN-Testing_0-190** VM Network. These VMs will be needed to demonstrate PVLAN functionality. It is recommended to use the following names for each of the additional VMs:

    ❑ `PVLAN190-2`

    ❑ `PVLAN190-3`

    ❑ `PVLAN190-4`

    It is advised to have all of these VMs on the same Hyper-V host unless your networking equipment has been configured with the same PVLANs and is PVLAN-capable.

21. Once the VMs have been deployed to the Hyper-V hosts, open a PowerShell console on the VMM server. Note that this does not need to be an elevated PowerShell console.

22. Once you have opened PowerShell, type in `Enter-PSSession HYPVCH1` and press *Enter* (where `HYPVCH1` is the name of the Hyper-V host where PVLAN190-1 is running).

23. As in the previous recipe, you will see the PowerShell session change.

```
Windows PowerShell
Copyright (C) 2013 Microsoft Corporation. All rights reserved.

PS C:\Users\adminuser> Enter-PSSession HYPVCH1
[HYPVCH1]: PS C:\Users\AdminUser\Documents>
```

24. The prefix **[HYVCH1]** indicates that any further PowerShell you execute in this console will be executed on HYPVCH1 until you exit the remote PowerShell session.

25. Enter the following PowerShell and press *Enter*:

```
Get-VMNetworkAdapterVlan -VMName PVLAN190-1
```

26. The following output will be returned:

```
[HYPVCH1]: PS C:\Users\AdminUser\Documents> Get-VMNetworkAdapterVlan -VMName PVLAN190-1

VMName       VMNetworkAdapterName Mode     VlanList
------       -------------------- ----     --------
PVLAN190-1   PVLAN190-1           Isolated 190,5
```

27. This shows the network adapter of **PVLAN190-1** to be in isolated mode as expected.

28. Keep this PowerShell console open as it will be needed shortly.

29. Ensure that VMs **PVLAN190-1** and **PVLAN190-2** are on the same host and are running.

30. Navigate to the **Fabric** workspace and click on **Logical Networks**.

31. On the ribbon bar, click on **Virtual Machines**.

32. In the filter enter `pvlan`.

33. You should then see four VMs.

Logical Network Information for Virtual Machines (4)		
pvlan		
Name	Type	Logical Netw...
⊞ PVLAN190-1	VM	
⊞ PVLAN190-2	VM	
⊞ PVLAN190-3	VM	
⊞ PVLAN190-4	VM	

34. By clicking on the **+** symbol you will see all of the network adapters attached to the VM and the IP address(es) that have been assigned.

Name	Type	Logical Netw...	IP Pool	IP Address
⊟ PVLAN190-1	VM			
PVLAN190-1	vNIC	PVLAN Testing	IPP-PVLAN_Testing_0-1...	192.168.190.2

35. Make a note of all four IP addresses. You may have a list similar to the following:

    ❑ **PVLAN190-1**: **192.168.190.2**
    ❑ **PVLAN190-2**: **192.168.190.3**
    ❑ **PVLAN190-3**: **192.168.190.6**
    ❑ **PVLAN190-4**: **192.168.190.5**

36. Ensure that each VM's firewall is either disabled or that the Windows Firewall rule **File and Printer Sharing (Echo Request - ICMPv4-In)** is enabled on each PVLAN virtual machine.

Promiscuous and Isolated

Perform the following steps for Promiscuous and Isolated modes:

1. In the VMM console, navigate to **VMs and Services** | **All Hosts** and enter PVLAN in the filter. For this part of the recipe, you will need the following VMs running:

    ❑ PVLAN190-1
    ❑ PVLAN190-2

2. Right-click on **PVLAN190-1**, navigate to **Connect or View**, and click on **Connect via Console**.

3. Log on to the VM using the default password.

4. Open an elevated PowerShell console.

5. Enter the following PowerShell and press *Enter*:

```
Test-NetConnection 192.168.190.3
```

Here, `192.168.190.3` is the IP address for PVLAN190-2.

6. This should fail and you should receive the following message in the PowerShell console:

```
WARNING: Ping to 192.168.190.3 failed -- Status: DestinationHostUnreachable

ComputerName              : 192.168.190.3
RemoteAddress             : 192.168.190.3
InterfaceAlias            : Ethernet 2
SourceAddress             : 192.168.190.2
PingSucceeded             : False
PingReplyDetails (RTT)    : 0 ms
```

7. If you do not receive this message, then please ensure that your PVLANs are configured correctly and that all of your PVLAN VMs are in isolated mode.

8. Repeat the process from PVLAN190-2 to PVLAN190-1 (steps 38-43). You should receive similar results.

```
WARNING: Ping to 192.168.190.2 failed -- Status: DestinationHostUnreachable

ComputerName              : 192.168.190.2
RemoteAddress             : 192.168.190.2
InterfaceAlias            : Ethernet 2
SourceAddress             : 192.168.190.3
PingSucceeded             : False
PingReplyDetails (RTT)    : 0 ms
```

9. This result shows how two VM network adapters that are in Isolated mode cannot communicate despite being on the same Primary and Secondary VLAN.

10. Using the PowerShell console that was left open on the VMM server in step 28, enter the following cmdlet (if this was closed please repeat steps 21-23):

```
Set-VMNetworkAdapterVlan –VMName PVLAN190-1 -Promiscuous -
    PrimaryVlanId 190 -SecondaryVlanIdList 5
```

11. Then, run the following PowerShell cmdlet:

```
Get-VMNetworkAdapterVlan -VMName PVLAN190-1
```

12. You will see that the mode has changed from Isolated to Promiscuous.

13. Repeat steps 40-43 and you will see that the VMs can now communicate:

```
PS C:\Users\Administrator> Test-NetConnection 192.168.190.2

ComputerName            : 192.168.190.2
RemoteAddress           : 192.168.190.2
InterfaceAlias          : Ethernet 2
SourceAddress           : 192.168.190.3
PingSucceeded           : True
PingReplyDetails (RTT)  : 1 ms
```

14. This shows how a VM network adapter that is in Isolated mode and one that is in Promiscuous mode can communicate on the same Primary and Secondary VLAN.

15. The PVLAN virtual machines should currently be in the following configuration:

Virtual Machine	PVLAN Mode
PVLAN190-1	Promiscuous
PVLAN190-2	Isolated
PVLAN190-3	Isolated
PVLAN190-4	Isolated

The following diagram shows this configuration:

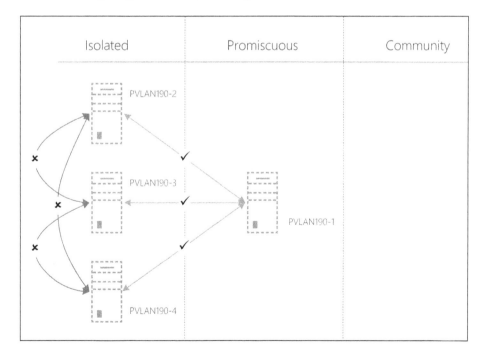

Promiscuous and Community

Perform the following steps for Promiscuous and Community modes:

1. In the VMM console, navigate to **VMs and Services | All Hosts** and enter PVLAN in the filter. For this part of the recipe you will need the following VMs running:

   ❑ **PVLAN190-1**

   ❑ **PVLAN190-2**

   ❑ **PVLAN190-3**

2. Right-click on **PVLAN190-1**, navigate to **Connect or View** and click on **Connect via Console**.

3. Log on to the VM using the default password.

4. Open an elevated PowerShell console.

5. Enter the following PowerShell and press *Enter*:

   ```
   Test-NetConnection 192.168.190.6
   ```

6. This should succeed and you should receive this message in the PowerShell console:

```
PS C:\Users\Administrator> Test-NetConnection 192.168.190.6

ComputerName              : 192.168.190.6
RemoteAddress             : 192.168.190.6
InterfaceAlias            : Ethernet 2
SourceAddress             : 192.168.190.2
PingSucceeded             : True
PingReplyDetails (RTT)    : 1 ms
```

7. In the VMM Console right-click on **PVLAN190-3**, navigate to **Connect or View**, and click on **Connect via Console**.

8. Log on to the VM using the default password.

9. Open an elevated PowerShell console.

10. Enter the following PowerShell and press *Enter*:

    ```
    Test-NetConnection 192.168.190.3
    ```

11. This should fail and you should receive the following message in the PowerShell console:

```
PS C:\Users\Administrator> Test-NetConnection 192.168.190.3
WARNING: Ping to 192.168.190.3 failed -- Status: DestinationHostUnreachable

ComputerName              : 192.168.190.3
RemoteAddress             : 192.168.190.3
InterfaceAlias            : Ethernet 2
SourceAddress             : 192.168.190.6
PingSucceeded             : False
PingReplyDetails (RTT)    : 0 ms
```

12. So the Isolated VMs cannot communicate with each other, but they can communicate with the VMs set to Promiscuous.

13. On the VMM server, open a PowerShell console. Note that this does not need to be an elevated PowerShell console.

14. Once you have opened PowerShell, type in `Enter-PSSession HYPVCH1` and press *Enter* (where `HYPVCH1` is the name of the Hyper-V host where PVLAN190-1 is running).

15. As in the previous recipe, you will see the PowerShell session change.

16. Using this PowerShell console enter the following cmdlet (if this was closed please repeat steps 21-23):

```
Set-VMNetworkAdapterVlan -VMName PVLAN190-3 -Community -
    PrimaryVlanId 190 -SecondaryVlanId 5
```

17. Then, run the following PowerShell cmdlet:

```
Get-VMNetworkAdapterVlan -VMName PVLAN190-3
```

18. You will see that the mode has changed from Isolated to Community. If you repeat steps 53-62, you will receive the same results, as there are now three VMs in use, one of each type.

19. The PVLAN virtual machines should currently be in the following configuration:

Virtual Machine	PVLAN Mode
PVLAN190-1	Promiscuous
PVLAN190-2	Isolated
PVLAN190-3	Community
PVLAN190-4	Isolated

The following diagram shows this configuration:

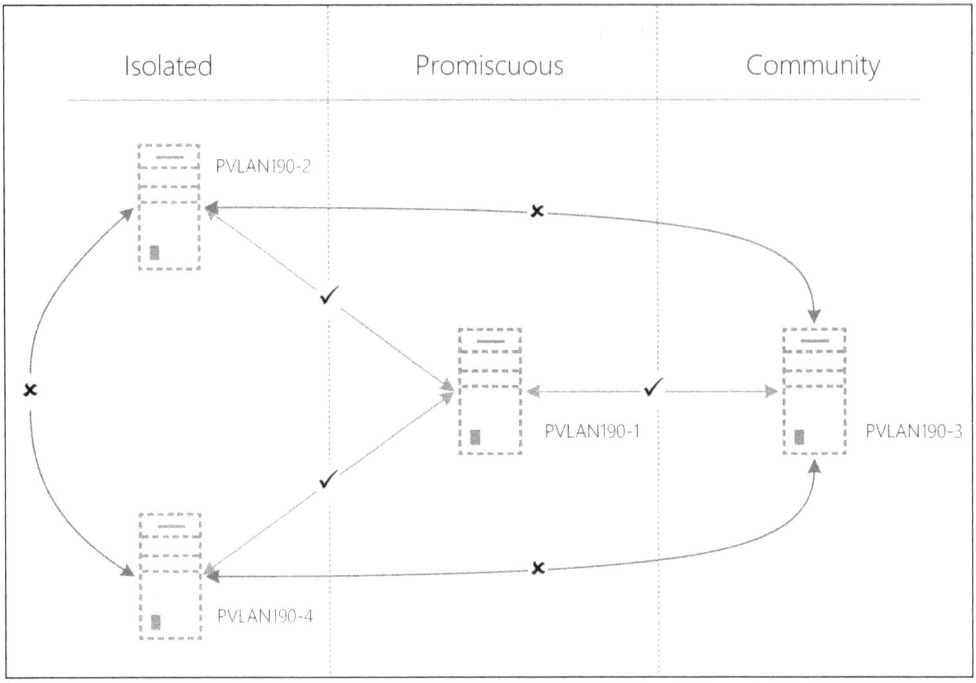

Promiscuous, Community, and Isolated

Perform the following steps for Promiscuous, Community, and Isolated modes:

1. In the VMM console, navigate to **VMs and Services** | **All Hosts** and enter PVLAN in the filter. For this part of the recipe you will need the following VMs running:

   ❑ **PVLAN190-1**

   ❑ **PVLAN190-2**

   ❑ **PVLAN190-3**

   ❑ **PVLAN190-4**

2. Right-click on **PVLAN190-1**, navigate to **Connect or View**, and click on **Connect via Console**.

3. Log on to the VM using the default password.

4. Open an elevated PowerShell console.

5. Enter the following PowerShell and press *Enter*:

   ```
   Test-NetConnection 192.168.190.5
   ```

6. This should succeed and you should receive the following message in the PowerShell console:

```
PS C:\Users\Administrator> Test-NetConnection 192.168.190.5

ComputerName            : 192.168.190.5
RemoteAddress           : 192.168.190.5
InterfaceAlias          : Ethernet 2
SourceAddress           : 192.168.190.2
PingSucceeded           : True
PingReplyDetails (RTT)  : 0 ms
```

7. In the VMM Console right-click on **PVLAN190-4**, navigate to **Connect or View**, and click on **Connect via Console**.

8. Log on to the VM using the default password.

9. Open an elevated PowerShell console.

10. Enter the following PowerShell and press *Enter*:

```
Test-NetConnection 192.168.190.6
```

11. This should fail and you should receive the following message in the PowerShell console:

```
PS C:\Users\Administrator> Test-NetConnection 192.168.190.6
WARNING: Ping to 192.168.190.6 failed -- Status: DestinationHostUnreachable

ComputerName            : 192.168.190.6
RemoteAddress           : 192.168.190.6
InterfaceAlias          : Ethernet 2
SourceAddress           : 192.168.190.5
PingSucceeded           : False
PingReplyDetails (RTT)  : 0 ms
```

12. On the VMM server open a PowerShell console. Note that this does not need to be an elevated PowerShell console.

13. Once you have opened PowerShell, type in `Enter-PSSession HYPVCH1` and press *Enter* (where `HYPVCH1` is the name of the Hyper-V host where PVLAN190-1 is running).

14. As in the previous recipe you will see the PowerShell session change.

```
                                                        Windows PowerShell
Windows PowerShell
Copyright (C) 2013 Microsoft Corporation. All rights reserved.

PS C:\Users\adminuser> Enter-PSSession HYPVCH1
[HYPVCH1]: PS C:\Users\AdminUser\Documents>
```

15. Using this PowerShell console enter the following cmdlet (if this was closed please repeat steps 21-23):

```
Set-VMNetworkAdapterVlan -VMName PVLAN190-4 -Community -
    PrimaryVlanId 190 -SecondaryVlanId 5
```

16. Then, run the following PowerShell cmdlet:

```
Get-VMNetworkAdapterVlan -VMName PVLAN190-4
```

17. You will see that the mode has changed from Isolated to Community.

18. This means that PVLAN190-4 can communicate with PVLAN190-1 and PVLAN190-4.

19. In the VMM Console, right-click on **PVLAN190-4**, navigate to **Connect or View**, and click on **Connect via Console**.

20. Log on to the VM using the default password.

21. Open an elevated PowerShell console.

22. Enter the following PowerShell cmdlets one at a time and press *Enter*:

```
Test-NetConnection 192.168.190.2
Test-NetConnection 192.168.190.3
Test-NetConnection 192.168.190.6
```

23. You should have the following results:

```
PS C:\Users\Administrator> Test-NetConnection 192.168.190.2


ComputerName            : 192.168.190.2
RemoteAddress           : 192.168.190.2
InterfaceAlias          : Ethernet 2
SourceAddress           : 192.168.190.5
PingSucceeded           : True
PingReplyDetails (RTT)  : 5 ms


PS C:\Users\Administrator> Test-NetConnection 192.168.190.3
WARNING: Ping to 192.168.190.3 failed -- Status: DestinationHostUnreachable


ComputerName            : 192.168.190.3
RemoteAddress           : 192.168.190.3
InterfaceAlias          : Ethernet 2
SourceAddress           : 192.168.190.5
PingSucceeded           : False
PingReplyDetails (RTT)  : 0 ms


PS C:\Users\Administrator> Test-NetConnection 192.168.190.6


ComputerName            : 192.168.190.6
RemoteAddress           : 192.168.190.6
InterfaceAlias          : Ethernet 2
SourceAddress           : 192.168.190.5
PingSucceeded           : True
PingReplyDetails (RTT)  : 2 ms
```

24. This shows that PVLAN190-4 can communicate with the VMs that are not isolated. The PVLAN virtual machines should be currently in the following configuration:

Virtual Machine	PVLAN Mode
PVLAN190-1	Promiscuous
PVLAN190-2	Isolated
PVLAN190-3	Community
PVLAN190-4	Community

The following diagram shows this configuration:

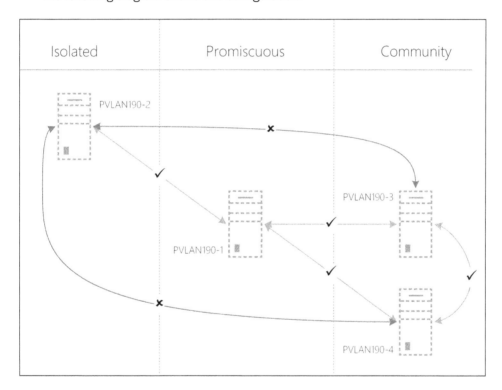

How it works...

Private VLANs are implemented within the Hyper-V Extensible Switch with the port configuration saved into the Virtual Machine's configuration file. Layer 2 traffic is controlled via the switch as the Hyper-V Extensible Switch understands the configuration of a PVLAN and its port type. The port type controls which devices within a PVLAN can communicate with one another.

7
Network Access Control Lists

In this chapter, we will cover the following recipes:

- ▶ Locking down a VM for security access
- ▶ Applying rules to a list of VMs

Introduction

In Windows Server 2012, Microsoft introduced the Hyper-V Extensible Switch. One of its features was the **Port Access Control List (ACL)**. This does not refer to a protocol port such as the TCP port for HTTP, but rather the logical port inside the Hyper-V Extensible Switch.

In Windows Server 2012 R2, Microsoft extended this functionality to include the following parameters:

- ▶ Source IP address
- ▶ Destination IP address
- ▶ Protocol
- ▶ Source port
- ▶ Destination port
- ▶ Direction (inbound/outbound)

As the configuration of the ACL relates to the VM, it is stored in the VM's configuration file. This ensures that if the VM is migrated to a different host, the ACLs will move with it.

System Center 2012 R2 VMM is not capable of managing ACLs for virtual machines, so the only option for managing ACLs is PowerShell.

Locking down a VM for security access

This recipe will show you how to apply ACLs to VMs to protect them from unauthorized access.

Getting ready

You will need to start two VMs in the **Tenant A** VM Network: in this case, **Tenant A – VM 10** (which was used in *Chapter 5, Windows Server Gateway Configuration*, to test the gateway and as such should have IIS installed) and **Tenant A – VM 11**.

How to do it...

The following diagram shows the high-level steps involved in this recipe:

```
Overview of Recipe:
  ┌────────────────────────────────────────────────┐
  │ Prerequisites (not covered by this recipe):      │
  │  • Complete Chapter 5                            │
  │  • Start two VMs in the same Tenant VM Network   │
  └────────────────────────────────────────────────┘

  ┌────────────────────────────────────────────────┐
  │ Actions:                                         │
  │  • Creation of Hyper-V Port ACLs                 │
  │  • Creation of Stateful Hyper-V Port ACLs        │
  │  • Testing of Port ACLs                          │
  └────────────────────────────────────────────────┘
```

Now perform the following steps:

1. In the VMM console, click on the **Home** tab in the ribbon bar and click on the **PowerShell** button. This will launch PowerShell with the VMM module already loaded and the console connected to the current VMM instance. To obtain the Virtual Subnet IDs for all subnets in the Tenant A VM Network, enter the following PowerShell:

    ```
    $VMNetworkName = "Tenant A"

    $VMNetwork = Get-SCVMNetwork | Where-Object -Property Name
      -EQ $VMNetworkName

    Get-SCVMSubnet -VMNetwork $VMNetwork | Select-Object
      VMNetwork,Name,SubnetVlans,VMSubnetID
    ```

2. You will be presented with the list of subnets and the `VMSubnetID` for each. The `VMSubnetID` will used later in this recipe; in this case, the `VMSubnetID` is **4490741**, as shown in the following screenshot:

 Your VMSubnetID value may be different to the one obtained here; this is normal behavior.

3. In the PowerShell Console, run the following PowerShell to get the IP addresses of Tenant A – VM 10 and Tenant A – VM 11:

```
$VMs  = @()
$VMs += Get-SCVirtualMachine -Name "Tenant A - VM 10"
$VMs += Get-SCVirtualMachine -Name "Tenant A - VM 11"

ForEach($VM in $VMs){
    Write-Output "$($VM.Name): $($VM.VirtualNetworkAdapters.
IPv4Addresses)"
    Write-Output "Host name: $($VM.HostName)"
}
```

4. You will be presented with the IPv4 addresses for the two VMs as shown in the following screenshot:

Please leave this PowerShell console open.

 Your IP addresses and host names may differ from those shown here; this is normal behavior.

5. In the VMM console, open the **VMs and Services** workspace and navigate to **All Hosts | Hosts | hypvclus01**.

6. Right-click on **Tenant A – VM 11**, navigate to **Connect or View**, and then click on **Connect via Console**.

7. Log in to the VM via the Remote Console.

8. Open Internet Explorer and go to the URL `http://10.0.0.14`, where 10.0.0.14 is the IP address of Tenant A – VM 10, as we discussed in step 4.

9. You will be greeted with the default IIS page. This shows that there are currently no ACLs preventing **Tenant A – VM 11** accessing **Tenant A – VM 10** within Hyper-V or within the Windows Firewall.

10. Open a PowerShell console on **Tenant A – VM 11** and enter the following command:

```
Ping 10.0.0.14 -t
```

11. Here, `10.0.0.14` is the IP address of **Tenant A – VM 10**. This will run a continuous ping against **Tenant A – VM10**.

12. In the PowerShell console left open in Step 4, enter the following PowerShell:

```
Invoke-Command -ComputerName HYPVCH1.ad.demo.com -
  ScriptBlock{
    Add-VMNetworkAdapterExtendedAcl -Action Deny -Direction
      Inbound -VMName "Tenant A - VM 10" -Weight 1 -
        IsolationID 4490741
}
```

Here, `HYPVCH1.ad.demo.com` is the name of the host where Tenant A – VM 10 is running, as obtained in step 4 and the `Isolation ID` needs to be set to the **VMSubnetID** as obtained in step 2.

Please leave this PowerShell console open.

 When adding base rules such as a Deny All, it is suggested to apply a weight of 1 to allow other rules to override it if appropriate.

13. Return to the PowerShell console left open on Tenant A – VM 11 in step 10. You will see that Tenant A – VM 10 has stopped responding to pings.

```
PS C:\Users\Administrator> ping 10.0.0.14 -t

Pinging 10.0.0.14 with 32 bytes of data:
Reply from 10.0.0.14: bytes=32 time=2ms TTL=128
Reply from 10.0.0.14: bytes=32 time<1ms TTL=128
Reply from 10.0.0.14: bytes=32 time<1ms TTL=128
Reply from 10.0.0.14: bytes=32 time<1ms TTL=128
Reply from 10.0.0.14: bytes=32 time<1ms TTL=128
Reply from 10.0.0.14: bytes=32 time<1ms TTL=128
Reply from 10.0.0.14: bytes=32 time=1ms TTL=128
Reply from 10.0.0.14: bytes=32 time=1ms TTL=128
Reply from 10.0.0.14: bytes=32 time<1ms TTL=128
Reply from 10.0.0.14: bytes=32 time<1ms TTL=128
Request timed out.
Request timed out.
Request timed out.
Request timed out.
```

This has created a Hyper-V Port ACL that will deny all inbound traffic to Tenant A – VM10.

14. In the same PowerShell console, enter the following PowerShell:

```
Test-NetConnection -CommonTCPPort HTTP -ComputerName
    10.0.0.14 -InformationLevel Detailed
```

15. Here, 10.0.0.14 is the IP address of Tenant A – VM 10. This shows that you cannot access the IIS website on Tenant A – VM 10.

```
PS C:\Users\Administrator> Test-NetConnection -CommonTCPPort HTTP -ComputerName 10.0.0.14 -InformationLevel Detailed
WARNING: Ping to 10.0.0.14 failed -- Status: TimedOut
WARNING: TCP connect to 10.0.0.14:80 failed

ComputerName              : 10.0.0.14
RemoteAddress             : 10.0.0.14
RemotePort                : 80
AllNameResolutionResults  :
MatchingIPsecRules        :
NetworkIsolationContext   : Private Network
InterfaceAlias            : Ethernet 2
SourceAddress             : 10.0.0.15
NetRoute (NextHop)        : 0.0.0.0
PingSucceeded             : False
PingReplyDetails (RTT)    : 0 ms
TcpTestSucceeded          : False
```

16. Return to the PowerShell console left open on the VMM console in step 11 and enter the following PowerShell cmdlets:

```
Invoke-Command -ComputerName HYPVCH1.ad.demo.com -
    ScriptBlock{
        Add-VMNetworkAdapterExtendedAcl -Action Allow -
            Direction Inbound -VMName "Tenant A - VM 10" -Weight
                10 -IsolationID 4490741 -LocalPort 80
}
```

Here, `HYPVCH1.ad.demo.com` is the name of the host where Tenant A – VM 10 is running, as obtained in step 4, and the `Isolation ID` needs to be set to **VMSubnetID** as obtained in step 2.

Please leave this PowerShell console open.

 When adding rules it is suggested to use weight increments of 10 to allow other rules to be inserted between rules if necessary.

17. On Tenant A – VM 11, repeat step 13. You will see that **TCPTestSucceeded** has changed to **True**.

18. Return to the PowerShell console left open on the VMM console in step 14, and enter the following PowerShell cmdlets:

```
Invoke-Command -ComputerName HYPVCH1.ad.demo.com -
  ScriptBlock{
    Add-VMNetworkAdapterExtendedAcl -Action Deny -Direction
      Outbound -VMName "Tenant A - VM 10" -Weight 1 -
        IsolationID 4490741
}
```

Here, `HYPVCH1.ad.demo.com` is the name of the host where Tenant A – VM 10 is running, as obtained in step 4, and the `Isolation ID` needs to be set to **VMSubnetID** as obtained in step 2.

Please leave this PowerShell console open.

 When adding base rules such as a Deny All, it is suggested to apply a weight of 1 to allow other rules to override it if appropriate.

19. On Tenant A – VM 11 repeat step 14. You will see that **TCPTestSucceeded** has changed to **False**. This is because all outbound connections have been denied.

20. Return to the PowerShell console left open on the VMM console in step 17, and enter the following PowerShell cmdlets:

```
Invoke-Command -ComputerName HYPVCH1.ad.demo.com -
  ScriptBlock{
    Remove-VMNetworkAdapterExtendedAcl -Direction Inbound -
      VMName "Tenant A - VM 10" -Weight 10
}
```

This removes the inbound rule for port 80. In the same PowerShell console enter the following cmdlets:

```
Invoke-Command -ComputerName HYPVCH1.ad.demo.com -
  ScriptBlock{
    Add-VMNetworkAdapterExtendedAcl -Action Allow -
      Direction Inbound -VMName "Tenant A - VM 10" -Weight
        10 -IsolationID 4490741 -LocalPort 80 -Stateful
          $True -Protocol TCP
}
```

This adds a stateful ACL rule; this ensures that the switch dynamically creates an outbound rule to allow the traffic to return to the requestor.

21. On Tenant A – VM 11 repeat step 14. You will see that the **TCPTestSucceeded** has changed to **True**. This is because the stateful ACL is now in place.

How it works...

Extended ACLs are applied as traffic ingresses and egresses the VM into and out of the Hyper-V switch. As the ACLs are VM-specific, they are stored in the VM's configuration file. This ensures that the ACLs are moved with the VM ensuring continuity of the ACL.

For the complete range of options, it is advisable to review the *TechNet* article at `http://technet.microsoft.com/en-us/library/dn464289.aspx`.

Applying rules to a list of VMs

Hyper-V supports a variety of operating systems, including those that do not have inbuilt firewalls like Windows Server 2012 R2. Using the Hyper-V Extended ACLs, you can provide basic levels of protection to these guest virtual machines.

Additionally, it may be a case that some users do not necessarily lock down their servers as much as the company requires. This can be typical of a short-lived server such as a test server.

Through the use of PowerShell, it is possible to apply a large number of Port ACLs to virtual machines quickly and efficiently.

This recipe will show you how to use a CSV file and PowerShell to apply a set of Port ACLs to multiple virtual machines.

Getting ready

This recipe uses a CSV file and it is recommended to create this in Microsoft Office Excel; having access to a computer with it installed would be beneficial.

How to do it...

The following diagram shows the high-level steps involved in this recipe:

Overview of Recipe:

Actions:
- Use PowerShell to apply a numerous Port ACLs listed in a CSV to multiple VMs

Now perform the following steps:

1. In Excel, create a new workbook.

2. Enter the following in row 1, one value per column:
   - ☐ `Action`
   - ☐ `Direction`
   - ☐ `Weight`
   - ☐ `LocalPort`
   - ☐ `Protocol`

3. The following table shows the content of the CSV file that will be used in this recipe:

Action	Direction	Weight	LocalPort	Protocol
Deny	Inbound	1		
Deny	Outbound	1		
Allow	Inbound	10		1
Allow	Inbound	20	80	TCP
Allow	Inbound	30	443	TCP
Allow	Outbound	10		1

 Protocol 1 refers to ICMP traffic such as Ping. TCP port 80 is typically HTTP and port 443 is typically HTTPS.

As you can see, there are two default rules to deny all inbound and outbound communication.

4. The PowerShell script at the end of this recipe accepts a CSV file and a list of VM names to apply the Port ACLs to. This script is a basic script to help you understand how the concept could work on a larger scale.

5. In the VMM console, click on the **Home** tab in the ribbon bar and click on the **PowerShell** button. This will launch PowerShell with the VMM module already loaded and the console connected to the current VMM instance.

6. In the PowerShell console, run the `Add-MultipleVMNetworkAdapterExtended Acl.ps1` script file using a copy of the CSV file shown in step 3 as the value for the parameter `CSVPath` and using `Tenant A - VM 10;Tenant A - VM 11` as the value for the parameter `VMList`. The code is as follows:

```
.\Add-MultipleVMNetworkAdapterExtendedAcl.ps1 -CSVPath
  .\Rules.csv -VMList "Tenant A - VM 10;Tenant A - VM 11"
```

How it works...

The PowerShell script (see the following section) parses the CSV file that is passed to it and creates rules for each entry in the file against each VM passed into the list. The script creates the PowerShell it is going to run as each rule could be different.

It is possible to take this script and extend its functionality to include a variety of other parameters, including IP addresses (both local and remote) and specific network adapters.

The Add-MultipleVMNetworkAdapterExtendedAcl.ps1 script

The content of Add-MultipleVMNetworkAdapterExtendedAcl.ps1 is as follows:

```
<#
.Synopsis
   Applies Hyper-V Extended Port ACLs to a number of VMs
.DESCRIPTION
  This script accepts a path to a CSV file where the rule
    definitions are listed and a list of VM names.
  It iterates through each VM applying the rules from the CSV
    file.
.PARAMETER CSVPath
  The location of the CSV that contains the rules to apply. Please
    see the Hyper-V Network Virtualization Cookbook
  for an example of the format used
.PARAMETER VMList
  This should contain a list of VMs to applt the rules to. You can
    pass an array such as @("VM 1","VM 2") or a ; separated list
      such as "VM 1;VM 2"
.EXAMPLE
   Add-MultipleVMNetworkAdapterExtendedAcl -CSVPath .\Rules.csv -
     VMList "Tenant A - VM 12;Tenant A - VM 13"
#>
[CmdletBinding()]

    Param
    (
        # CSVPath is the path to the CSV containing the rules
        [Parameter(Mandatory=$true,
                   Position=0)]
        [ValidateNotNull()]
        [ValidateNotNullOrEmpty()]
        [ValidateScript({
            #Ensure the CSV file exists
```

```
            Test-Path -Path $_ -PathType Leaf
    })]
    [string] $CSVPath,

    # VMList is the list of VMs to applt the port ACLs to
    [Parameter(Mandatory=$true,
               Position=1)]
    [ValidateNotNull()]
    [ValidateNotNullOrEmpty()]
    [string[]] $VMList
)

Begin
{
    Write-Verbose "Starting process"
    Write-Verbose "Importing CSV file $CSVPath"
    #Read in the CSV containing the Port ACL list
    $PortRules = Import-Csv -Path $CSVPath

    if($VMList[0].contains(";")){
        Write-Verbose "Found at least one ; in the VMList.
            Changing to an array"
        $VMList = $VMList.Split(";")
    }


 }
Process
{
    #Build PowerShell cmdlet to execute against remote server
        for VM
    $BaseLine = "Add-VMNetworkAdapterExtendedAcl -Action {0} -
        Direction {1} -VMName ""{2}"" -Weight {3} -IsolationID
            {4}"
    $StatefulBase = " -LocalPort {0} -Protocol {1} -Stateful
        `$True"

    #Iterate each VM in the list the user has passed
    Write-Verbose "Iterating through each VM in VMList"
    ForEach($VM in $VMList){
        #Get the VM from VMM
        Write-Verbose "Getting information for
            ""$($VM.Trim())"" from VMM"
```

```
$VmmVm = Get-SCVirtualMachine -Name $VM.Trim()

#Check if VMM has found something
if(-Not($VmmVm)){
    Write-Error "$VM cannot be found in VMM"
    #Move to the next VM in the list
    continue;
}


#Determine the VM Network VM Subnet ID
Write-Verbose "Getting Virtual Subnet ID for
    ""$($VM.Trim())"""
$VMSubnetID = (Get-SCVMSubnet -VMNetwork
  $VmmVM.VirtualNetworkAdapters.VMNetwork -Name
    $VmmVM.VirtualNetworkAdapters.VMSubnet).VMSubnetID
Write-Verbose "Virtual Subnet ID is: $VMSubnetID"
#Build a list of rules to run
$RulesToRun = ,@()

#Iterate each rule the user has defined
Write-Verbose "Iterating through each Rule to apply
  building complete list to apply. There are
    $($PortRules.Count) to apply."
ForEach($Rule in $PortRules){

    #Format the baseline of the rule to add the basic
      rule parameters
    $ExprToRun = $BaseLine -f
      $Rule.Action,$Rule.Direction,$VmmVm.Name,$Rule.
        Weight,$VMSubnetID

    #Is it ICMP traffic?
    If($Rule.Protocol -eq "1"){
        $ExprToRun += " -Protocol 1"
    }elseif($Rule.Protocol){
        #Make it stateful
        $ExprToRun += $StatefulBase -f
          $Rule.LocalPort,$Rule.Protocol
    }
    #Add to the list
    $RulesToRun += $ExprToRun
}

#Execute the rules on the remote host
```

```
            Write-Verbose "Adding rules to ""$($VM.Trim())"" using
              remote Powershell on VM host ""$($VmmVm.HostName)"""
            Invoke-Command -ComputerName $VmmVm.HostName -
              ScriptBlock{
                #Get the Rules to process
                Param(
                    [string[]]$Rules
                )
                #Iterate each rule
                ForEach($Rule in $Rules){
                    #Check the rule is not blank
                    if($Rule){
                        Invoke-Expression $Rule
                    }
                }

            } -ArgumentList (,$RulesToRun) #the (,<VAR>) syntax
                ensures the variable is passed as an array

            Write-Verbose "Process complete for ""$($VM.Trim())"""

        }

    }
    End
    {
        Write-Verbose "Process complete"
    }
```

VM Templates

The recipes in this book use a simple **Virtual Machine Template** (**VM Template**). It was created using the `Convert-WindowsImage.ps1` PowerShell script. This script can be downloaded from `https://gallery.technet.microsoft.com/scriptcenter/ Convert-WindowsImageps1-0fe23a8f`.

This script is capable of creating a VHDX file from a **Windows Imaging File Format (WIM)** file; the `install.wim` file was sourced from the Windows Server 2012 R2 ISO file.

The following screenshot shows how the VHDX file was created:

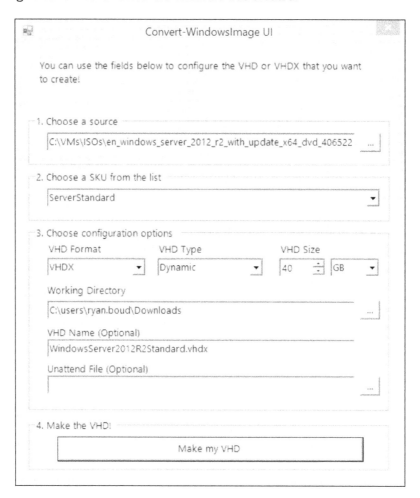

The VHDX file was added to a new Virtual Machine and the setup of Windows was completed. This gave a basic installation of Windows Server 2012 R2 Standard for the recipes in this book.

Configuration

After the completion of the setup process, the following PowerShell cmdlets were executed on the virtual machine in an elevated PowerShell console:

```
#Enable SMB IN, ICMP ECHO IPv4
$FileSharing = ("FPS-SMB-In-TCP","FPS-ICMP4-ERQ-In")
$FileSharing | %{ Enable-NetFirewallRule -Name $_}

#Required WMI rules
$WMI = ("WMI-ASYNC-In-TCP","WMI-RPCSS-In-TCP","WMI-WINMGMT-In-
  TCP")
$WMI | %{ Enable-NetFirewallRule -Name $_}

#Enable PowerShell Remoting
Enable-PSRemoting -Force
```

These cmdlets enable the following Firewall rules:

- ▸ File and Printer Sharing (SMB-In)
- ▸ File and Printer Sharing (Echo Request - ICMPv4-In)
- ▸ Windows Management Instrumentation (ASync-In)
- ▸ Windows Management Instrumentation (DCOM-In)
- ▸ Windows Management Instrumentation (WMI-In)

By enabling these Firewall rules within the VM template, any VM created using this template will automatically have these rules enabled. Additionally, the PowerShell cmdlets ensure that PowerShell Remoting is enabled.

Sysprep

The virtual machine was sysprep'd using the following command line in an elevated command prompt:

```
C:\Windows\System32\Sysprep\sysprep.exe /Generalize /Oobe /Shutdown /
mode:VM
```

After the VM shutdown, the VHDX file was used to create the Domain Controller, VMM Servers, SQL Servers, and the VMM Library Servers. Once VMM was operational, it was copied into the VMM Library for the recipes in this book.

Planning the Virtual Machine Manager

The installation of **Virtual Machine Manager** (**VMM**) is quite simple; however, you must plan your deployment. This appendix details the elements you must take into consideration before proceeding with the installation.

Preparing

It is recommended that you read through the latest release notes for VMM on the Microsoft TechNet located at `http://technet.microsoft.com/en-us/library/dn303329.aspx`. Microsoft updates the release notes as and when required.

How to plan the Virtual Machine Manager

When planning the VMM, it is vital to understand the architecture of the network that VMM and Hyper-V will be operating on, the availability requirements for VMM, the types of storage infrastructure involved, and the technology involved (VMM and Hyper-V).

To understand the architecture of the network is to understand the scale of the solution required. If you have two host servers and some basic iSCSI storage infrastructure, then your challenges will be different compared to an organization with 200 host servers with complex Fibre Channel or Scale-Out File Server storage implementations. Typically, this will involve:

- ▶ Architectural diagrams of the network
- ▶ The VLANs in use
- ▶ The IP subnets in use

- ▸ The gateway infrastructure
- ▸ The location of domain controllers
- ▸ The storage architecture

If you have two servers or do not have a complication Hyper-V Network Virtualization, then VMM may not be a critical component. For enterprises implementing HNV, VMM becomes a critical application or for service providers implementing a multitenancy environment with the Windows Azure Pack. Typically, this will involve:

- ▸ Documenting low-level requirements for the VMM implementation
- ▸ Understanding the implications of a failure of VMM
- ▸ Realizing the technologies available to your organization (SQL AlwaysOn High Availability Groups)

The storage you have may impact the architecture of the VMM and Hyper-V design. For example, if you have Fibre Channel or Fibre Channel over Ethernet storage, then you may be able to create Virtual SANs. If you are using Scale-Out File Servers, then you might be able to leverage SMB Direct. Typically, this will involve:

- ▸ A deep understanding of the storage infrastructure in your enterprise
- ▸ Realizing the options your storage presents to you (for example, shared VHDX, CSV caching, storage tiering, and so on)

Planning for the technology involved and where it will be deployed in your infrastructure will involve where VMM servers are to be located and the number and types of availability required:

- ▸ All of the information gained in the previous steps will be used to determine the requirements of the deployment

The different deployment types are described in the following table:

Deployment type	Description
Single server	This has a single point of failure, all on one VM or physical server. This also has the test environment and demo lab. This is supported in production, but it is not scalable.
Multiserver	In this type of deployment, the components of VMM are installed on separate servers that could be highly available.

The minimum requirements for each component of VMM 2012 R2 are covered in the following table:

Component	Minimum requirements
VirtualManagerDB	**Software**: ▸ SQL Server 2008 R2 SP2 (Standard, Enterprise, or Datacenter) or later, with the Database Engine Services and Management Tools (complete features) **Hardware**: ▸ Dual-core, 64-bit, 2 GHz CPU processor ▸ 4 GB RAM ▸ 150 GB of HDD space on which the operating system is installed ▸ 50 GB of HDD space on which the database is stored
Management Server	**Software**: ▸ Windows Server 2012 or higher (Standard or Datacenter) ▸ .NET Framework 4.5 or 4.5.1 ▸ Windows Remote Management (WinRM) service ▸ Windows ADK (Deployment tools and Windows preinstallation environment) ▸ SQL Server 2008 R2 Command Line Utilities or SQL Server 2012 Command Line Utilities, depending on which version of SQL Server you install **Hardware**: ▸ Pentium 4, 64-bit, 2 GHz CPU processor ▸ 4 GB RAM ▸ 2 GB of HDD space (without a local SQL install) ▸ 80 GB of HDD space (with a local SQL install)

Component	Minimum requirements
VMM Console	**Software:** ▸ Any x86 or x64 version of Windows 7 SP1 (Professional, Enterprise, or Ultimate editions), or Windows 8/8.1 (Professional or Enterprise) ▸ Windows Server 2008 R2 SP1 (Standard, Enterprise, or Datacenter), Windows Server 2012 (Standard or Datacenter), or Windows Server 2012 R2 (Standard or Datacenter) ▸ Windows PowerShell 3.0 (included in Windows 8 and Windows Server 2012 and higher) ▸ .NET Framework 4, 4.5, or 4.5.1 ▸ The console must be installed on an active directory domain joined computer **Hardware:** ▸ Pentium 4, 2 GHz CPU processor ▸ 2 GB RAM ▸ 2 GB of HDD
VMM Library	**Software:** ▸ Windows Server 2008 R2 SP1 (Standard, Enterprise, or Datacenter), Windows Server 2012 (Standard or Datacenter), or Windows Server 2012 R2 (Standard or Datacenter) ▸ WinRM 2.0 or higher **Hardware:** ▸ Pentium 4, 2.8 GHz CPU processor ▸ 2 GB RAM ▸ The amount of HDD space varies on the content to be stored but 50 GB as minimum is recommended

Component	Minimum requirements
PXE Server	**Software**: ▸ Windows Server 2008 R2 SP1 (Standard, Enterprise, or Datacenter), Windows Server 2012 (Standard or Datacenter), or Windows Server 2012 R2 (Standard or Datacenter) ▸ The Windows Deployment Services Role must be installed ▸ WinRM 2.0 or higher Please note that configuration of the WDS role is not required as VMM uses its own PXE provider. **Hardware**: ▸ Pentium 4, 2.8 GHz CPU processor ▸ 2 GB RAM ▸ The amount of HDD space varies on the content to be stored but 10 GB as minimum is recommend
Update Server	**Software**: ▸ A 64-bit edition of Windows Server Update Services (WSUS) 3.0 Service Pack 2 ▸ A 64-bit edition of WSUS server role on Windows Server 2012 or Windows Server 2012 R2 ▸ VMM can use either a WSUS root server or a downstream WSUS server; it does not support the use of a WSUS replica server ▸ VMM supports using a WSUS server that is part of a Configuration Manager 2007 R2 or System Center 2012 Configuration Manager environment, but additional configuration steps are required ▸ If you do not install WSUS server on the same computer as the VMM management server, you must install a WSUS Administrator Console on the VMM management server **Hardware**: ▸ **Windows Server 2008 R2**: 1.4 GHz (x64 processor), 512 MB RAM, 20 GB HDD space ▸ **Windows Server 2012 and higher**: 1.4 GHz (x64 processor), 512 MB RAM, 32 GB HDD space

The required service accounts are as follows:

Account name	Used for	Description
VMM service account	Running VMM services and accessing resources	This is a domain account that requires local administrator privileges on VMM servers.
VMM Agent run as account	Managing Hyper-V hosts	This is a domain account that requires local administrator privileges on VMM servers. This account also requires delegated rights in the domain to Create Computer Objects and Read All Properties to allow new Hyper-V hosts to be joined to the existing cluster.
VMM SQL Server account	Running VMM SQL Server Instance	This is a domain account.
VM SQL Server account	SQL Service account when installing SQL from Service Template	This is a domain account.
Local administrator run as account	Setting the Local Administrator name and password during a build	This is a local account.
VM Domain Join run as account	Joining new VMs to the domain	This is a domain account with delegated rights to Add Computer to Domain.
IPMI account	Controlling the lights out card during a bare metal build	This account needs the ability to connect to a server and also power on and off the server.

Network Communication Ports are as follows:

Purpose	Protocol	Port number(s)	Where to change
VMM management server to WSUS server (data channel)	HTTP/HTTPS	80/8530 (non-SSL), 443/8531 (with SSL)	These ports are the IIS port binding with WSUS. They cannot be changed from VMM.
VMM management server to WSUS server (control channel)	HTTP/HTTPS	80/8530 (non-SSL), 443/8531 (with SSL)	These ports are the IIS port binding with WSUS. They cannot be changed from VMM.
BITS port for VMM transfers (data channel)	BITS	443	This port is changed when the VMM is set up.

Purpose	Protocol	Port number(s)	Where to change
VMM library server to hosts file transfer	BITS	443 (maximum value: 32768)	This port is changed when the VMM is set up.
VMM host-to-host file transfer	BITS	443 (maximum value: 32768)	
VMM management server to in-guest agent (VMM to virtual machine data channel)	HTTPS	443 (maximum value: 32768)	This port is changed using BITS.
VMM management server to VMM agent on Windows server-based host (data channel for file transfers)	HTTPS	443 (maximum value: 32768)	This port is changed using BITS.
VMM management server to remote Microsoft SQL Server database	TDS	1433	
Console connections (RDP) to virtual machines through Hyper-V hosts (VMConnect)	RDP	2179	This port is changed using the VMM console.
Remote Desktop to virtual machines	RDP	3389	This port is changed on the virtual machine.
VMM management server to VMM agent on Windows server-based host (control channel)	WS-Management	5985	This port is changed when the VMM is set up.
VMM management server to in-guest agent (VMM to virtual machine control channel)	WS-Management	5985	
VMM management server to VMM agent on Windows server–based host (control channel—SSL)	WS-Management	5986	
VMM console to VMM management server	WCF	8100	This port is changed when the VMM is set up.

Purpose	Protocol	Port number(s)	Where to change
VMM console to VMM management server (HTTPS)	WCF	8101	This port is changed when the VMM is set up.
Windows PE agent to VMM management server (control channel)	WCF	8101	This port is changed when the VMM is set up.
VMM console to VMM management server (NET.TCP)	WCF	8102	This port is changed when the VMM is set up.
WDS provider to VMM management server	WCF	8102	This port is changed when the VMM is set up.
VMM console to VMM management server (HTTP)	WCF	8103	This port is changed when VMM is set up.
Windows PE agent to VMM management server (time sync)	WCF	8103	This port is changed when the VMM is set up.
VMM management server to Cluster PowerShell interface	PowerShell		

The most critical elements in these tables are the networking layouts. For Hyper-V Network Virtualization, you need to ensure the VLANs and subnets in use are large enough to cope with the required workloads for your environment.

It is absolutely critical that all the information is collated and the scope and purpose of the installation is formalized and agreed upon. This ensures that all involved parties can understand their required work items and participation in the project.

Index

Thank you for buying

Hyper-V Network Virtualization Cookbook

About Packt Publishing

Packt, pronounced 'packed', published its first book "*Mastering phpMyAdmin for Effective MySQL Management*" in April 2004 and subsequently continued to specialize in publishing highly focused books on specific technologies and solutions.

Our books and publications share the experiences of your fellow IT professionals in adapting and customizing today's systems, applications, and frameworks. Our solution-based books give you the knowledge and power to customize the software and technologies you're using to get the job done. Packt books are more specific and less general than the IT books you have seen in the past. Our unique business model allows us to bring you more focused information, giving you more of what you need to know, and less of what you don't.

Packt is a modern, yet unique publishing company, which focuses on producing quality, cutting-edge books for communities of developers, administrators, and newbies alike. For more information, please visit our website: www.PacktPub.com.

About Packt Enterprise

In 2010, Packt launched two new brands, Packt Enterprise and Packt Open Source, in order to continue its focus on specialization. This book is part of the Packt Enterprise brand, home to books published on enterprise software – software created by major vendors, including (but not limited to) IBM, Microsoft and Oracle, often for use in other corporations. Its titles will offer information relevant to a range of users of this software, including administrators, developers, architects, and end users.

Writing for Packt

We welcome all inquiries from people who are interested in authoring. Book proposals should be sent to author@packtpub.com. If your book idea is still at an early stage and you would like to discuss it first before writing a formal book proposal, contact us; one of our commissioning editors will get in touch with you.

We're not just looking for published authors; if you have strong technical skills but no writing experience, our experienced editors can help you develop a writing career, or simply get some additional reward for your expertise.

Windows Server 2012 Hyper-V Cookbook

ISBN: 978-1-84968-442-2   Paperback: 304 pages

Over 50 simple but incredibly effective recipes for mastering the administration of Windows Server Hyper-V

1. Take advantage of numerous Hyper-V best practices for administrators.

2. Get to grips with migrating virtual machines between servers and old Hyper-V versions, automating tasks with PowerShell, providing a high availability and disaster recovery environment, and much more.

3. A practical Cookbook bursting with essential recipes.

Windows Server 2012 Hyper-V: Deploying Hyper-V Enterprise Server Virtualization Platform

ISBN: 978-1-84968-834-5   Paperback: 410 pages

Build Hyper-V infrastructure with secured multitenancy, flexible infrastructure, scalability, and high availability

1. A complete step-by-step Hyper-V deployment guide, covering all Hyper-V features for configuration and management best practices.

2. Understand multitenancy, flexible architecture, scalability, and high availability features of new Windows Server 2012 Hyper-V.

Please check **www.PacktPub.com** for information on our titles

Instant Hyper-V Server Virtualization Starter

ISBN: 978-1-78217-997-9   Paperback: 58 pages

An intuitive guide to learning Virtualization with Hyper-V

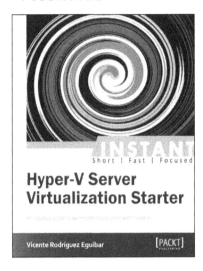

1. Learn something new in an Instant! A short, fast, focused guide delivering immediate results.

2. Step-by-step, practical guide to understanding and implementing Virtualization for an enterprise environment.

3. Learn how to create a virtual machine in three steps.

4. Learn about capacity planning, virtual network management, integrating your virtual host, and more.

Hyper-V Replica Essentials

ISBN: 978-1-78217-188-1   Paperback: 96 pages

Ensure business continuity and improve your disaster recovery policy using Hyper-V Replica

1. A practical step-by-step guide that goes beyond theory and focuses on getting hands-on.

2. Ensure business continuity and faster disaster recovery.

3. Learn how to deploy a failover cluster and encrypt communication traffic.

Please check **www.PacktPub.com** for information on our titles

www.ingramcontent.com/pod-product-compliance
Lightning Source LLC
Chambersburg PA
CBHW060551060326
40690CB00017B/3673